G000047479

NEW CLASSICS

For my inspirational Ma, Bet.
Thank you for planting the seed x

Published in 2013 by Hardie Grant Books

Hardie Grant Books (Australia)
Ground Floor, Building 1
658 Church Street
Richmond, Victoria 3181
www.hardiegrant.com.au

Hardie Grant Books (UK)
Second Floor, North Suite
Dudley House, Southampton Street
London WC2E 7HF
www.hardiegrant.co.uk

All rights reserved. No part of this publication may be reproduced, stored
in a retrieval system or transmitted in any form by any means, electronic,
mechanical, photocopying, recording or otherwise, without the prior written
permission of the publishers and copyright holders.

The moral rights of the author have been asserted.

Copyright text © Philippa Sibley 2013
Copyright photography © Mark Roper 2013
Copyright author photograph © Fiona Brook 2013
Copyright design © Hardie Grant Books 2013

A Cataloguing-in-Publication entry is available from the catalogue of the
National Library of Australia at www.nla.gov.au
New Classics
ISBN 9781742705408

Publishing director: Paul McNally
Project editor: Ariana Klepac
Design manager: Heather Menzies
Design concept: Tonto Design
Design layout and paper artist: Aileen Lord
Photographer: Mark Roper
Stylist: Leesa O'Reilly
Production: Todd Rechner

Printed in China by 1010 Printing International Limited
Colour reproduction by Splitting Image Colour Studio

PHILIPPA SIBLEY
NEW CLASSICS

hardie grant books

MELBOURNE · LONDON

CONTENTS

FOREWORD

I've known Philippa since we worked together in a Fitzroy pub some time last century and so I have been a fan, a friend and a follower for more years than either of us would like committed to paper. One of the things that I've always appreciated about her is the refreshing no-nonsense, straight-talking honesty that is as present in her cooking as it is in her personality. She's the arch foe of pretentiousness and so it is with a little trepidation that I make a statement that she would never, ever make about herself.

Philippa is an artist.

I can feel her cringing already but it's true. And I don't just say artist because of her wide renown for creating some of the most beautiful, complex, magnificently flavoured desserts you could ever sink your teeth into, though they are certainly part of the picture and of her talents.

I say artist because she is truly creative and original but still manages to make food that you want to eat. There's no dust and dehydration, no gas and powder in her approach.

Instead there are dishes that are based in solid, tried and true combinations of the tomatoes and basil variety, that she then reinterprets, tweaks, adds new twists to and turns upside down so that she emerges with something that's comforting and recognisable but also completely fresh. She re-imagines. She re-considers.

This is why *New Classics* is a perfect name for this book because it really captures what Philippa does. With humour and wit, a generous sharing of hard-earned tips and advice, meticulous step-by-step instructions, stories of family and friends and beautiful photography, Philippa lucidly and candidly shares with us her passion and philosophy. Not to mention her sense of fun.

But best of all, she helps us reconnect with classic flavours and dishes by allowing us to see them with fresh eyes. And that, whether Philippa likes it or not, is the sign of a true artist.

Michael Harden

INTRODUCTION

I am often asked how I came up with a certain dish or combination: 'What was your inspiration for that?!'.

My original inspiration was my upbringing. My mother is, and has always been, a passionate and driven foodie and entertainer. When I was growing up, my parents' dinner parties were epic; the stuff of legend! Lavish, indulgent and well researched. Themed imaginatively and always with a sense of fun. Raw fish in the seventies. Pigeon pie! My father was a pigeon fancier … ahem. I remember a medieval feast to celebrate a play that Dad had been in (they were very theatrical folk) with the moniker 'Ye Olde Feast'. Featuring on the menu was 'swan pie' (goose substituted), and spotted dick for dessert. The guests were required to dress appropriately for the period. Pewter goblets were acquired. Authentic calligraphy was studied for the menu writing. Candles only. No detail amiss. It was such a hoot and, wow, the leftovers!

So began my love of entertaining. Luckily I became obsessed with cooking to match. I devoured cookbooks and magazines and demanded to take over at least half the week of cooking for the family. Dad would bemoan the fact that I was terrible at cleaning up and try and stifle my blossoming creativity, only to give in after a particularly delicious batch of cookies, declaring, 'Oh, what's the point? If she can't find anything to cook in the kitchen, she'll just go and pull up some grass and cook with that!'

Due to Mum's similar passion, our library was full of amazing, well-thumbed books on food. James Beard, Julia Childs, Robert Carrier and Elizabeth David were my first culinary heroes. Then in the eighties Stephanie Alexander hit the Melbourne food scene and I promised myself I'd be the Stephanie of the nineties. Stephanie is still the doyenne of those and the decade to come. She is a huge inspiration to me. One of her protégés, Tansy Good, also had a big effect on my career.

I was taken to 'Tansy's' in the late eighties for my birthday and still remember the meal. The dessert in particular rocked my world. It was a perfectly poached ripe yellow peach with a peach bavarois topped with a peach jelly of amazing flavour and clarity. I was besotted. Having only cooked casually in the odd pub here and there and having been disinclined to start an apprenticeship, I was excited to get a phone call from my over zealous (when it comes to food and cooking) mother. 'There's an ad in the paper!

Tansy's are looking for a "reasonably qualified chef"!' With youthful exuberance and no real idea I called and somehow managed to get an interview – despite the fact that Mum had misread 'recently' for 'reasonably'. I got the job! I can honestly say those were the most terrifying nine months of my young life. I was twenty years old, inexperienced and uppity. Man, did I learn a lot in a short time! Dispatching yabbies, and butchering hares, pheasants and lambs. Dashing upstairs to make pastry and cakes and service. The yelling, the speed, the expectations! And that was day one! Working with the wonderful Karen Martini and Rita Macali made it all worthwhile, though. I wish I'd recorded the debriefs.

Next came the infamous 1990 bestseller and trailblazer White Heat by Marco Pierre White. Pictures of the food and the rock star connotations aside, the main reason I was inspired by Marco was his laborious banging on about 'his boys' and how women shouldn't eat robust dishes because they are cleaner than men and need a cleaner diet. Then he'd describe his food as being 'feminine' and that he was a women's man. He liked women because they aren't competitive! I was determined to work for this dude and that I did. I still have the reference he (then rarely) wrote for me, just before I convinced his coveted head chef to move to France with me and then to Australia where we opened est est est, Luxe and then Ondine.

I must also mention, with huge respect and admiration, Michel Roux, a gentleman and scholar. I am on my fifth copy of his book Desserts: A Lifelong Passion. It was the inspiration for my book PS Desserts.

Thomas Keller and Heston Blumenthal have also been influential to me, as they respect the lessons learnt from the past and are especially 'old school' in their approach – tipping their hats to the classics while improving and putting new twists on them.

Marriages are precious when it comes to flavours – tomatoes and basil, chocolate and pear, poultry and mushrooms. I'm celebrating the tried and true, almost like covering a favourite song or remaking an unforgettable movie, with respect and love. Revisiting, though, not 'deconstructing'. No gels, foams or soils. I'm keeping it real and cooking what I'm good at – what I love to eat.

NOTES

GOLDEN RULES

1. Use the finest ingredients you can find and afford.

2. Believe in seasonality!

3. Find a good butcher and fishmonger and become friendly with them. You'll be surprised how helpful they can be.

4. Use eggs from happy chickens – organic and free-range when possible (for superior flavour and peace of mind).

5. Invest in good-quality equipment. Buy some heavy-based pots and pans, some good baking trays that will withstand high temperatures without buckling and a decent knife set and sharpening steel.

6. Read through the whole recipe before starting so you know what's involved in each step. Prepare what you can in advance to save time and stress.

7. Always preheat your oven as directed.

8. Trust your own instincts. Recipes are guides not gospel. If you think your pan is too hot and the meat is burning or something needs more time in the oven than the recipe states, take action. Season to taste. Touch for temperature. Feel for texture. Use your initiative.

9. Don't be disheartened if the recipe doesn't turn out perfectly. Learn from your mistakes. First and foremost, enjoy yourself!

10. If you don't know how to do something, look it up on the internet. There are plenty of useful, free step-by-step techniques videos to find there.

Notes on the recipes

The cream used in these recipes is 35 per cent butter fat.

All butter is unsalted.

Use salt flakes (coarse/kosher) salt to season.

Use freshly ground pepper.

Use extra-virgin olive oil for dressing and low-heat cooking only – it burns at quite a low temperature, so is inappropriate for frying. Use canola and vegetable oils for high-heat cooking and deep-frying. Use light olive oil for vinaigrettes and mayonnaise.

From left to right: fontina, crème fraîche, burrata, Persian feta, Fourme d'Ambert, haloumi, goat's curd, Parmigiano Reggiano, unsalted butter.

NOTES ON CHEESE AND DAIRY

I can't imagine life, cooking or eating, without dairy. I feel so sorry for the lactose-intolerant.

Australia is producing some wonderful artisan cheeses these days but I can't resist Parmigano Reggiano from Italy, French Roquefort and Cypriot haloumi. As an Australian I was amazed when I travelled to France and saw the huge variety of cheeses on offer both for sale in 'fromageries' and markets and on restaurant menus. Fresh and aged, made from cow's, goat's or sheep's milk and combinations of all three, beautifully and enticingly displayed everywhere. Many French cheeses are far too delicate to travel and our quarantine laws forbid certain unpasteurised products into Australia, so seeing the diversity and enormity of choice was a revelation to me.

The first time I dined in a restaurant in Paris and was presented with the cheese selection I was flabbergasted. 'Help yourself, Mademoiselle,' I was told by the waiter in English. What followed, in French, I can only assume was very disapproving to say the least – lesson learned; never cut the tip off a wedge of brie … sacrilege!

The French are extremely proud and respectful when it comes to their cheeses, as I am increasingly each year about our cheeses in Australia. Pyengana cheddar from Tasmania is a multi award-winning cheese and certainly one of the finest cheddars I've tasted anywhere. 'Holy Goat' in Victoria is producing goat's milk cheeses that rival the best chèvres from Europe.

The divine cultured butter made from Pepe Saya crème fraîche has changed my mind about Australian butters once and for all – not all Australian butters, mind you. Pepe Saya and many others are now producing creams and butters with clean, fresh flavours that I have previously struggled to find locally. My friends, family and colleagues will attest to my butter snobbery. They have often become frustrated at my refusal to serve, cook with or eat some of the more commonly available products, preferring imported butter for pastry and serving to customers.

When serving cheese, always remember to allow it to come to room temperature first. When choosing butter, always check the use-by date. It's made with cream and as such is very perishable. There is nothing worse than the flavour of rancid butter.

From left to right: wild rice, farro, basmati rice, spelt, quinoa,
black lentils, red quinoa.

NOTES ON GRAINS

The resurgence in popularity of seeds and grains can only be described as having been a long time coming. Referred to as 'ancient' and 'forgotten', the likes of freekeh (a type of green wheat), farro (a type of wheat), spelt (an ancient type of wheat) and quinoa (the seeds of a plant from the amaranth family) were barely seen in kitchens, domestic or commercial, until fairly recently – definitely not by me anyway.

Now these ingredients have become popular again, and rightly so. Aside from being incredibly high in protein, fibre and nutrients, they add unique flavours, texture and general goodness to our modern diet.

In soups, salads and for that 'farinaceous' element – that we associate with a well-rounded meal/dish – these long-lost grains are welcomed back and cherished again, putting us in touch with a slower, more natural, way of life.

From left to right: Swiss brown, grey ghost, king brown,
pine or saffron milk cap, shimeji, oyster, slippery Jack

NOTES ON MUSHROOMS

These days I wonder, considering all the native Australian mushrooms that are now available, how many delicious and perfectly non-toxic fungi I tramped on and kicked at in my gumboots as a kid.

Pine mushrooms – also known as saffron milk caps – slippery Jacks and grey ghosts are shuffled in through the back door at the restaurant by bearded, beanie-wearing chaps. The pine mushrooms are festooned with pine needles and sometimes feature the odd little nibble from some kind of marsupial or other … so they can't be poisonous.

These native mushrooms, like the divine European ceps, porcinis, chanterelles and morels, are very seasonal and dependent on ideal weather. The French refer to seeking out these treasures as 'la chasse', or the hunt. Mushroom hunters are very secretive about their sources, and with good reason. Superior specimens are sought after with passion and paid for accordingly.

I associate wild mushroom season with game and rich poultry such as pheasant, quail and partridge and the earthy flavours of tubers and roots, such as celeriac and Jerusalem artichokes.

In the last ten or so years, the variety of cultivated mushrooms you can find in stores has increased enormously. Asian mushrooms like oyster, enoki and shiitake, along with many others, are widely available. Pungent dried French and Italian varieties add richness to stocks and stews and, most excitingly, Australian truffle farmers are now providing us with this most magical and indulgent ingredient from our very own terroir. Who'd have ever thought the man that sells you fresh truffles would say 'G'day mate!'.

NOTES ON GARLIC

Garlic is at once one of the most revered and abhorred ingredients in the world but, along with salt and pepper, it is one of the most commonly used. Most countries' cuisines feature garlic. In fact, off the top of my head, I can't think of one cuisine that doesn't feature garlic.

I consider garlic as a staple – unsubstitutable. An ingredient that non-cooks take for granted – if it's not there, you'll notice something is missing but you may not know what. Raw, sautéed, roasted or confit, in sauces, stocks, dressings or marinades, garlic can be either the wallflower or the screaming queen of cooking.

I am a 'come lately' fan of the Korean preserved, black garlic. What an amazing product! Black as night, pungent but delicate, almost licorice-like, this product has inspired my repertoire and will continue to do so … find some now!

Roasting garlic in its skin, on rock salt and wrapped in foil produces the most beautiful purée. Squeeze the sweet flesh from the skins after baking for several hours and store in the refrigerator covered in a little extra-virgin olive oil for a warm soft garlicky hit in soups, mayonnaise or simply smeared on toast.

I'm pretty obsessive when it comes to raw garlic. I insist that if there is a green core or 'germ' in the garlic it has to be removed, as it imparts a really unpleasant bitter taste.

Hugely healthy and heady, garlic is definitely one of my 'can't live without' ingredients.

From left to right: chervil, chives, French tarragon, basil, bay, baby basil, thyme, fennel tips.

NOTES ON HERBS

As you will notice from the recipes in this book, I use lots of herbs in my cooking, and not only in savoury dishes. I divide herbs into two categories: hard and soft.

Hard herbs are robust and hearty and their fragrance and flavour stand up to long cooking times or, in fact, are improved by cooking. Thyme and bay are nearly always present in stocks and sauces, braises and stews. Thyme and bay, along with parsley, leek and celery, all tied together with butcher's twine, make up the 'bouquet garni' that you will often see in traditional French recipes. Sage, oregano and marjoram, like thyme and bay, are nearly always cooked or heated in some way and often removed after cooking, having imparted or infused their flavours – rather like tea.

Soft herbs, on the other hand, are more delicate plants and are better added to a dish near the end of the cooking, or used fresh and raw in salads and sauces.

Herbs such as chives and chervil make beautiful and flavoursome garnishes. Basil, with its spicy, aniseed flavour, complements a myriad of dishes from soups to sweets. If you do need to buy soft herbs, do so very near the time you will be using them as they don't last very long once cut.

My favourite herb is probably tarragon. James Beard said in his fabulous book *Delights and Prejudices* that if by chance he had to eat human, if tarragon was involved he may just do so! Chicken with tarragon is one of the great marriages. If you grow tarragon and find yourself with a bumper crop in late summer, get busy making tarragon butter and vinegar so you can enjoy its divine flavour all through the year.

Most herbs are available to buy in bunches at good food stores and markets but I love to grow my own. A bay tree, thyme and marjoram plants and a pot of basil in a sunny spot are a great start.

From left to right: cavolo nero, witlof (Belgian endive/chicory),
broad (fava) beans, purple witlof, borlotti (cranberry) beans,
flat beans, upland cress, black kale, leeks.

NOTES ON SPRING GREENS

Spring arrives early in Australia. Vegetables like broad (fava) beans, asparagus and globe artichokes appear sporadically and enticingly from late winter.

The seasons have created certain marriages in flavour, generally by serendipity. Broad beans, young leeks and artichokes together are a thing of beauty, especially when braised with a little saffron and white wine. The albeit small window of opportunity when Victorian morel mushrooms and new-season asparagus collide, provides inspiration for a myriad of dishes – from risotto to good old macaroni cheese.

Friendly salad

You can judge a cook by how she or he does the simple things. Choosing the freshest most vibrant lettuces and then carefully washing and drying them, so as not to damage the leaves, is actually not something that occurs naturally to some people. Then picking the choice inner bits and dressing at the very last minute before serving is crucial. I guess this is more of a philosophy than a recipe.

I scrutinise this dish more so than any other on my menu, much to the bemusement of my staff. They soon get the picture though. 'Not friendly enough!' I shout if I find a bruised or old, outside leaf in the bowl, or 'Too bloody friendly; it's practically humping my leg!', if the bowl is overstuffed or overdressed.

The name comes from my lyrical and loud-mouthed brother David, who would bemoan the presence of bitter leaves in salads at family gatherings, stating he only wanted 'the friendly bits'.

The dressing I use is a very simple and old-fashioned vinaigrette – crush 1 garlic clove (germ removed) with 1 teaspoon salt using a mortar and pestle. Add 1 tablespoon dijon mustard. Transfer to a medium-sized bowl and add 100 ml (3½ fl oz) each lemon juice and sherry (or white wine vinegar). Grind in some white pepper then whisk in 400 ml (13½ fl oz) extra-virgin olive oil. Check the seasoning. You won't need this amount all at once but it keeps in the refrigerator for up to a week. Just take it out of the refrigerator for a while before use and shake well to re-emulsify.

My favourite leaves and lettuces to use are butter, oak leaf, iceberg and witlof (Belgian endive/chicory). Watercress and upland cress are also beautiful additions. The leaves should be bite-sized, spankingly crisp and dressed so they glisten but don't wilt.

From left to right: kipfler (fingerling) potatoes, brussels sprouts, celeriac, Jerusalem artichokes, fennel, parsnip, pumpkin (winter squash), beetroot (beets), celery, chestnuts.

NOTES ON WINTER VEGETABLES

The cold months bring wonderful diversity, with earthy root vegetables and tubers, such as parsnips, beetroot (beets) and Jerusalem artichokes. Try these thinly sliced and deep-fried and seasoned well with salt flakes for amazing and unusual crisps.

Potatoes, from large to tiny, are at their best in winter. Large floury potatoes like royal blue or desiree make beautiful mash and light, fluffy gnocchi. Tiny cocktail potatoes, such as kipfler (fingerling), and the charmingly named pink fir apple variety, are ideal for boiling and serving steaming hot or in salads.

Pumpkin (winter squash) and the gnarly celeriac inspire me to make hearty soups and purées. Common celery, too, is in its prime in winter. You'll notice that its stalks are longer, paler and generally more crunchy.

Brussels sprouts and fennel are delicious both cooked and raw. Try swapping cabbage with very finely shaved brussels sprouts next time you make coleslaw.

Buy chestnuts when they first appear, and take the time to roast and peel them while they're still plump and ripe. I love to use these treasures in both savoury dishes and desserts. Remember that they are a fruit and therefore do have a shelf life. Chestnuts freeze very well so get them while they're hot, so to speak.

From left to right: quinces, blueberries, blood plums, raspberries,
pink lady apple, fuji apple, golden delicious apple, bartlett pears.

NOTES ON FRUIT

Fresh fruits in season are probably my favourite ingredients, and I use them in both sweet and savoury dishes. In Melbourne, where I live, seasonality really does dictate quality. I find it quite romantic that many fruits are only available when they are in season – for me this evokes memories and associations. When the first cherries appear, I think of the coming summer and all the beautiful stone fruits I so enjoy using at Christmas time. Then come the blackberries, plums and figs in autumn. In winter, orchard fruits, quinces, apples and pears are in their prime as are all the citrus – mandarins, lemons, blood oranges and ruby grapefruits always feature on my menus in the colder months.

Use your senses when choosing fruits. Smell strawberries and other berries – if they are fragrant they will inevitably taste wonderful. Check the bottom of the punnet, as often underripe or squashed fruit will be stashed underneath the nice-looking fruit. It may come as a surprise to some, but strawberries are very good, if not at their best, in the winter months, especially those from Queensland. When choosing melons, feel for weight and firmness. Pineapples are ripe when they have a golden hue at the base and the leaves pluck out easily. When checking peaches and plums for ripeness, always press gently near where the stalk is, as you don't want to bruise the fruit on its presentation side. Pears are tricky. I suggest buying firm, green, slightly underripe pears and letting them ripen for several days at room temperature before using.

Fruits are fragile ingredients, so treat them with care. Don't leave stone fruits all jumbled up in bags on top of each other as they will likely bruise or become damaged and this will affect their final presentation.

BASICS

These are my 'go to' recipes – storable, freezable standbys, great to master as a part of your repertoire. Good stocks are essential building blocks for soups, sauces and for braising. Béchamel sauce is one of the mother sauces of French cuisine, and is used in many recipes, such as lasagne and as a base for cheesy sauces. Mayonnaise is simple to make and very versatile. The pâte sucrée recipe is really easy to work with, unlike some others I have used. It's pliable and strong but tender and crisp when baked. It keeps refrigerated for weeks. Pre-roll a tart shell and keep it in the freezer so you can turn out a beautiful fruit tart in just hours. Crème anglaise can be poured cold over fruits or warm over puddings. It also churns into divine ice creams.

This basic stock is used in many recipes throughout the book. Even if you only need a little for a particular recipe, make a decent amount and freeze the remainder in 500 ml (17 fl oz/2 cup) batches so you can whip up something else at the drop of a hat.

Makes about 3 litres (101 fl oz/12 cups)

CHICKEN STOCK

5 chicken carcasses, roughly chopped with a cleaver

1 leek, white part only, split lengthways and rinsed

3 celery stalks

1 large brown onion, peeled and quartered

2 sprigs of thyme

1 bay leaf

stalks from 1 bunch of parsley

1 tablespoon white peppercorns

1. Rinse the chicken carcasses in cold water and remove any really fatty bits from the birds.

1

2. Place the chicken pieces in a large deep saucepan or stockpot and cover them with cold water. Bring to the boil over medium heat. Using a ladle, skim off any matter that rises to the surface.

3. Add the leek, celery, onion, thyme, bay leaf, parsley and peppercorns to the saucepan.

4. Reduce the heat to low and allow the stock to simmer, skimming off the fat regularly, for 4 hours.

5. Remove the saucepan from the heat and allow to cool slightly for about 20 minutes, then gently pour or ladle the stock through a fine sieve into another pan or bowl. Either use immediately for your chosen recipe, or allow to cool completely before refrigerating or freezing. The stock will keep in the refrigerator for 3–4 days and freezes for 6 weeks, or even longer in a consistent deep freeze.

5

In this stock recipe, chicken wings and bones are cooked in the oven to caramelise, and then cooked on the stovetop in regular chicken stock, resulting in a richer, darker, more complex stock.

Makes about 1.5 litres (51 fl oz/6 cups)

DOUBLE CHICKEN STOCK

1 kg (2 lb 3 oz) chicken wings

3 chicken carcasses, chopped roughly with a cleaver

200 ml (7 fl oz) cooking oil

2 litres (68 fl oz/8 cups) Chicken stock (see page 34)

300 ml (10 fl oz) dry white wine

1. Rinse the chicken wings well in a colander under cold running water.

2. Preheat the oven to 200°C (400°F).

3. Mix the chicken wings with the other bones, toss in the oil and transfer them to a large baking tray. Roast the wings and bones until dark golden brown, shaking the tray occasionally during cooking.

4. Remove the tray from the oven. Transfer the bones to a heavy-based saucepan. Tip out any excess fat from the tray, then add the wine and deglaze the tray on the stovetop, scraping up any crispy bits stuck to the bottom. Add this mixture to the saucepan with the bones.

5. Add enough chicken stock to just cover the bones. Over high heat, bring the liquid up to the boil, skimming off any matter that rises to the surface as you go, then reduce the heat to low and allow to simmer for 4 hours.

6. Remove the pan from the heat and allow to cool.

7. Gently ladle the stock through a fine sieve and portion it into even batches to store. The stock will keep in the refrigerator for 3–4 days and freezes for 6 weeks, or even longer in a consistent deep freeze.

5 | 7

This stock is created using lamb bones and flavoured with herbs and vegetables. Use it for meatier recipes, such as the Roasted rack of lamb recipe on page 188.

Makes about 2 litres (68 fl oz/8 cups) light stock and 800 ml (27 fl oz) rich, reduced stock

LAMB STOCK

4 kg (8 lb 13 oz) lamb back bones, sawn into 4 cm (1½ in lengths) (you can ask your butcher to do this for you)

4 garlic bulbs, halved crossways

6 marjoram sprigs

Mirepoix

1 large brown onion, peeled and chopped

2 carrots, chopped

1 leek, white part only, split lengthwise, rinsed, and chopped

4 celery stalks, chopped

bouquet garni

2 tablespoons vegetable or canola oil

2 litres (68 fl oz/8 cups) Chicken stock (see page 34) or water

1. Preheat the oven to 200°C (400°F).

2. Spread out the lamb bones evenly in a large shallow baking tin, and add the garlic bulb halves and marjoram sprigs. Roast for about 30 minutes or until the bones are dark golden brown, shaking the tin occasionally during cooking.

3. Sauté the mirepoix vegetables in a large heavy-based saucepan or stockpot with the bouquet garni and the oil over high heat for 8–10 minutes until browned.

4. Add the roasted lamb bones, garlic and marjoram to the saucepan and mix with the vegetables.

5. Add the chicken stock or water to just cover the bones. Bring to the boil, skimming off any impurities as you go. Reduce the heat and allow to simmer on low for 4 hours.

6. Remove the saucepan from the heat and allow to cool.

7. Gently ladle the stock through a fine sieve and portion into even batches to store. The stock will keep in the refrigerator for 3–4 days and freezes for 6 weeks, or even longer in a consistent deep freeze.

Use béchamel sauce, cheesy or otherwise, for gratins or layered between pasta sheets with sautéed spinach and roasted pumpkin (winter squash) for an extravagant vegetarian lasagne.

Makes about 600 g (1 lb 5 oz)

BÉCHAMEL SAUCE

2 cloves

1 small brown onion, peeled and halved

500 ml (17 fl oz/2 cups) full-cream (whole) milk

4 sprigs of thyme

1 bay leaf

1 garlic clove, crushed

60 g (2 oz) butter

60 g (2 oz) plain (all-purpose) flour

Infusing the milk
1. Push the cloves into the onion and place the onion in a saucepan with the milk, herbs and garlic. Bring the mixture to the boil over medium heat then reduce the heat and allow to simmer for a few minutes. Remove from the heat and allow to infuse for 10 minutes.

1

Making the roux

2. Meanwhile, melt the butter in a medium saucepan over medium heat and add the flour. Stir with a wooden spoon until the mixture starts to bubble and lighten in colour. Continue to cook for a few minutes but don't allow the mixture to brown. This mixture is known as your 'roux'.

Finishing the sauce

3. Strain the milk through a sieve into a pitcher and remove and discard the onion, herbs and garlic.

4. Pour a little of the milk into the roux mixture in the saucepan, stirring all the time with a wooden spoon.

5. Switch to a hand whisk and continue adding the milk, little by little, until it has all been absorbed. Continue to cook for several minutes over medium heat, whisking constantly, until the béchamel is thick and smooth.

6. Pour the béchamel sauce into a mixing bowl and cover with baking paper or plastic wrap, making contact with the surface of the sauce, to prevent a skin from forming. Set aside until needed.

This is a basic mayonnaise recipe. Add chopped herbs, capers and cornichons for a classic sauce tartare to serve with fish, or a little cider vinegar and a pinch of sugar for an awesome coleslaw dressing.

Makes about 500 g (1 lb 2 oz)

MAYONNAISE

2 egg yolks

1 whole egg

1 tablespoon dijon mustard

350 ml (12 fl oz) light olive oil, or a neutral oil, such as canola

1½ tablespoons water

salt and pepper

1 teaspoon white wine vinegar

lemon juice

1. Put the egg yolks, the whole egg and the dijon mustard in a food processor or blender and process until all the ingredients are well combined.

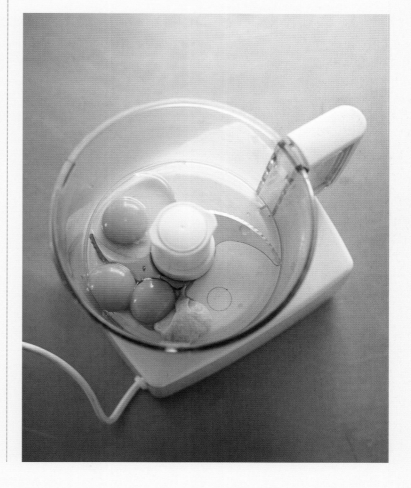

1

2. Start drizzling the light olive oil into the food processor in a thin stream, while the machine is running.

3. Add little splashes of cold water to the mixture as the mayonnaise begins to thicken.

4. When all the olive oil has been absorbed, season the mixture with salt and pepper and add the white wine vinegar and lemon juice to taste.

5. Pour the mayonnaise into a bowl and cover with baking paper or plastic wrap, making contact with the surface of the sauce, to prevent a skin from forming. Set aside until needed.

This sweet pastry is your dessert workhorse. Not only is it a delicious support act to many other ingredients, the pastry itself is not too 'short', so it's easy to work with. Short refers to the texture of the pastry. The more butter it has, the shorter or more delicate and crumbly it becomes.

Makes 1.1 kg (2 lb 7 oz)

PÂTE SUCRÉE

360 g (12½ oz) butter, softened

150 g (5½ oz) pure icing (confectioners') sugar, sifted

4 egg yolks, plus 1 extra lightly beaten egg yolk for brushing

2½ tablespoons cold water

500 g (1 lb 2 oz/3⅓ cups) plain (all-purpose) flour, plus extra for dusting

a pinch of cooking salt

Making the dough

1. Place the softened butter in the bowl of an electric mixer fitted with a paddle attachment. Work the butter on low speed until it is smooth and of a uniform texture.

1

2. Add the icing sugar and mix on medium speed until combined, taking care not to aerate too much – you don't want it to go pale and fluffy.

3. In a separate bowl, combine the 4 egg yolks and water. While still mixing, add to the butter mixture little by little. At this stage the mixture may look as though it has separated, but once the flour is added this will be rectified.

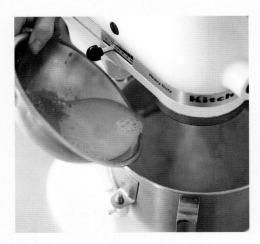

4. Now turn off the mixer and tip in the flour and salt. On low speed, work in the flour and salt until the mixture comes together and is crumbly. Do not overwork at this stage as the gluten in the flour will activate and the pastry could become tough.

4

Working the dough

5. Tip the contents of the bowl onto a work surface and, using the heel of your hand, smear the mixture away from you until it looks smooth and no patches of butter remain.

6. Using a palette knife or scraper, scrape the pastry together into a mound. Divide the mound of pastry in half and pat each half into about 3 cm (1¼ in) high rounds – you don't want a big boulder otherwise it will make it harder to achieve the right temperature to work the dough later. Wrap in plastic wrap and refrigerate until chilled all the way through.

7. Once the dough has chilled, remove it from the refrigerator and place on a work surface lightly dusted with flour. Chop the dough into manageable bits and smear each bit with the heel of your hand to get the dough going. If you missed any bits of butter before, make sure you smear them out this time.

8. Once the pastry dough is all of a uniform texture, bring it all together again.

9. Shape the pastry back into a ball and it's now ready to roll out and use. If you want to freeze this pastry, freeze at the end of Step 6. Remove from the freezer and thaw overnight in the refrigerator before rolling out.

Crème anglaise is basically custard. It may seem old-fashioned to make your own custard, but it is an essential part of a chef's artillery. From the four basic ingredients of milk, cream, sugar and egg yolks, pure magic happens. It adds a decadent finishing touch when served as a sauce to accompany simple fresh berries or churned into a luxe ice cream.

Makes 650 ml (22 fl oz)

CRÈME ANGLAISE

250 ml (8½ fl oz/1 cup) milk

250 ml (8½ fl oz/1 cup) thickened (whipping) cream

1 vanilla bean, split and seeds scraped out

100 g (3½ oz) caster (superfine) sugar

100 g (3½ oz) egg yolks (about 5)

1. Combine the milk and thickened cream in a saucepan with the vanilla bean and seeds and bring to a simmer over medium heat.

2. In a large mixing bowl, whisk the caster sugar into the egg yolks until the mixture is pale and thick.

1

3. Pour one-third of the hot milk mixture into the egg yolk mixture, whisking constantly. This 'tempers' or stabilises the egg yolk. If you add all the hot liquid at once, the yolks could 'shock' and curdle.

4. Pour the egg yolk mixture back into the pan with the milk and cream and place over medium heat. Stir constantly but gently and slowly with a wooden spoon, using a figure-eight movement, until the mixture begins to thicken and the bubbles disappear.

5. To test whether the crème anglaise is ready, lift the wooden spoon from the mixture and draw a line with your finger across the back of it. If the line remains distinct without liquid running into it for several seconds, it's ready. If you are unsure, use a thermometer and when the temperature reaches 80°C (176°F), it's ready.

6. Pour the crème anglaise into a bowl and place it over a larger bowl half-filled with iced water, to arrest the cooking. You will notice a slightly 'scrambled' appearance on the base of the pan. this indicates that the crème anglaise is cooked properly. Stir the anglaise regularly as it cools.

7. Once cooled, strain through a sieve into a bowl. It is now ready to serve or use as directed in your recipe. You can store the crème anglaise in the refrigerator for several days.

6
5

SMALL PLATES

These tasty, enticing morsels and titbits are designed to hand around at cocktail parties or present as a beautiful spread. They are guaranteed to please, both flavour-wise and visually. Many can be prepared well ahead of time and put together on the day of your gathering. I've included dishes for vegetarians, fish lovers and carnivores alike. I hope they become your portfolio of nibbles or finger food when it comes to entertaining. Both the falafel and arancini recipes give quite large yields, but they freeze well stored in airtight containers, so make the full amount and store for another occasion, if you're only having a few people over.

Using fresh broad beans instead of the more traditional dried, along with the fresh mint and coriander, gives an awesome colour that surprises when you bite into the dark golden brown shell. I like them spicy, but you can tone the heat down to suit your palate. The tangy lime and nutty yoghurt make these hot little gems an invigorating mouthful.

Serves 6

FRESH BROAD BEAN FALAFELS, TAHINI YOGHURT

Broad bean falafels

2 teaspoons cumin seeds

2 teaspoons coriander seeds

1 teaspoon white peppercorns

½ teaspoon cayenne pepper (or to taste)

400 g (14 oz/2⅔ cups) blanched broad (fava) beans (frozen broad beans can be substituted – no need to blanch them, just peel when defrosted)

200 g (7 oz/1⅓ cups) frozen peas

250 g (9 oz) cooked chickpeas (garbanzo beans) (or 400 g/14 oz tinned chickpeas, drained and rinsed)

1 small red onion, finely chopped

3 garlic cloves

1 or 2 small hot green bird's eye or scud chillies, deseeded

20 g (¾ oz/1 cup) firmly packed mint leaves

1 bunch of coriander (cilantro), stalks and roots intact, well rinsed

85 g (3 oz/⅔ cup) cornflour (cornstarch)

salt

Tahini yoghurt

250 g (9 oz/1 cup) plain yoghurt

1 tablespoon tahini

juice of 1 lemon

salt

For deep-frying

2 litres (68 fl oz/8 cups) canola oil

To serve

sea salt flakes

extra mint and coriander (cilantro) leaves and shoots (optional) for garnish

lime cheeks

black sesame seeds (optional)

For the falafels

1. Toast the cumin and coriander seeds and the white peppercorns in a frying pan over medium heat for several minutes, shaking the pan constantly, until the spices are fragrant. Allow to cool, then pulverise in a spice grinder or crush until very fine using a mortar and pestle. (If you use a mortar and pestle you may have to sieve the spices to remove any large pieces.)

2. Pop the broad beans from their shells.

For the tahini yoghurt

6. Mix all the tahini yoghurt ingredients together well and adjust the seasoning to your taste.

To deep-fry

7. Heat the oil in a deep-fryer or large deep saucepan to 180°C (350°F) or until the handle of a wooden spoon bubbles vigorously when dipped in the oil.

8. Deep-fry the falafels – in batches of 8 at a time, or you will cool down your oil too much. Cook until dark golden brown and very crisp, about 4–5 minutes.

3. Place all the remaining falafel ingredients, except the cornflour and salt, into a food processor (you will probably need to do this in batches) and process until fairly smooth, firm and spoonable.

4. Transfer the mixture to a bowl and stir the cornflour in thoroughly. Taste the mixture and adjust the seasoning. If you like it hot add more cayenne pepper.

5. Using 2 dessertspoons dipped in hot water, shape the mixture into quenelles and place on baking paper.

To serve

9. Drain the falafels on paper towel.

10. Season the falafels with salt flakes to taste and arrange them on your serving platter.

11. Scatter around the mint, coriander, lime cheeks and sesame seeds (if using) and serve the falafels hot with the tahini yoghurt on the side for dipping.

One of my first, and still one of my favourite risottos, was made with prawn bisque or stock. The rich flavour and deceptive simplicity was a revelation to me and was something I really wanted to perfect. What a crowd pleaser this would be! Years later, having pleased the crowds, I've taken it sideways and created these little 'bombs'. The black aïoli adds even more theatre, but they are still awesome with just a squeeze of lemon.

Makes 24

PRAWN AND SAFFRON ARANCINI, BLACK AÏOLI

Arancini base

12 raw prawns (shrimp)

1.5 litres (51 fl oz/6 cups) prawn (shrimp) stock (see marron stock recipe on page 174 for instructions)

1 small brown onion, very finely diced

125 ml (4 fl oz/½ cup) olive oil

250 g (9 oz) arborio rice

a large pinch of saffron threads

200 ml (7 fl oz) white wine

30 g (1 oz/½ cup) thinly sliced basil

salt and pepper

juice of 1 lemon

110 g (4 oz/½ cup) mascarpone or crème fraîche

150 g (5½ oz/1 cup) plain (all-purpose) flour

2 eggs whisked with 1 tablespoon milk

200 g (7 oz/2 cups) dry breadcrumbs

Peel and devein the prawns, leaving the last 1–1.5 cm (½ in) of shell and the tail. (You can use the shells for the stock.) Split the prawns lengthways and trim to about 4 cm (1½ in) long. Chop the trimmed pieces and refrigerate until needed.

Bring the stock to the boil over medium heat then reduce the heat and keep warm.

In a large heavy-based saucepan, sweat the onion in the olive oil until translucent. Add the rice and the saffron and continue cooking for several minutes to roast the rice. Pour in the white wine and cook, stirring continuously, until the wine has evaporated. Add the warm stock and cook, stirring often, for 15–20 minutes until the rice is cooked. (You are 'overcooking' as you need the mixture to be quite starchy so it holds together in balls.) Add the basil and season with salt and pepper and lemon juice to taste. Stir through the chopped prawn meat and mascarpone and spread onto a tray to cool.

Have three bowls at hand – one containing the flour, one with the egg mixture and one with the breadcrumbs.

Scoop about a tablespoon of the rice mixture into your hand and make a dent to put a half prawn into. Shape the mixture around the prawn into a ball, leaving the tail poking out like a little fuse. When you have used all the prawns, roll any remaining mixture into extra arancini. Gently roll each ball in the flour then dip in the egg and finally roll in the breadcrumbs. Put the arancini in the refrigerator until you are ready to cook them.

Black aïoli

1 garlic clove, peeled and roughly chopped

3 black garlic cloves (available at Asian grocers and good markets)

1 teaspoon dijon mustard

1 x 25 g (1 oz) sachet squid ink (available from some fishmongers) (optional)

2 egg yolks

300 ml (10 fl oz) light olive oil

1 tablespoon red wine vinegar

salt

lemon juice

green Tabasco

For deep-frying

2 litres (68 fl oz/8 cups) canola or other oil suitable for deep-frying

salt

baby basil leaves for garnish

To make the black aïoli, put the garlics, dijon mustard, squid ink (if using) and egg yolks in a blender and process until very smooth. With the motor running on medium speed, start drizzling in the oil in a thin stream. When half the oil is absorbed add the vinegar and then continue with the oil. If the mixture looks too thick add a splash of cold water. When all the oil is absorbed, season with salt, lemon juice and green Tabasco to taste.

To deep-fry, heat the oil in a large heavy-based saucepan or deep-fryer to 180°C (350°F) or until the handle of a wooden spoon bubbles vigorously when dipped in the oil. Deep-fry the arancini in batches of six or so until dark golden brown, about 3 minutes. Drain on paper towel. Sprinkle with salt. When all are cooked place each on a spoonful of the aïoli or serve the aïoli in a side dish. Garnish with a few basil leaves and serve while hot.

See photograph on page 78.

Prawn and saffron arancini,
black aïoli, page 76

Salmon pastrami, mussel, apple
and fennel salad, page 80

Spices very similar to those used to cure beef pastrami are used in this recipe, hence the name. This is a lovely, light dish. A crisp, sweet and aniseedy salad, flinty mussels and the classic accompaniments to salmon – rye bread and crème fraîche – tie all the flavours together beautifully.

Serves 8 generously

SALMON PASTRAMI, MUSSEL, APPLE AND FENNEL SALAD

1.5–2 kg (3 lb 5 oz–4 lb 6 oz) salmon fillet, skinned and pin-boned

Cure mix

100 g (3½ oz) fine pink lake salt

145 g (5 oz/⅔ cup) caster (superfine) sugar

10 g (¼ oz) black peppercorns, finely ground

10 g (¼ oz) coriander seeds, toasted and finely ground

Pastrami spice crust

40 g (1½ oz) black peppercorns

80 g (2¾ oz) coriander seeds, toasted

80 g (2¾ oz) yellow mustard seeds, toasted

For the cure mix, combine all the ingredients. On a tray appropriate to the size of the fish, spread over half the cure mix evenly, place the salmon on top and then cover the fish with the remaining cure mix. Cover with plastic wrap and place a tray on top to weight it down slightly. This will ensure the spices infuse well into the fish. Place in the refrigerator and leave to cure for 12 hours, then turn the fillet over on the tray and leave for another 12 hours. After 24 hours, scrape off the cure mix with the back of a knife and pat dry with paper towel.

Square up the salmon fillet so the fish is an even thickness.

For the pastrami spice crust, mix together the ingredients and grind coarsely in a spice grinder or using a mortar and pestle. Remove any lumps.

Press the spice crust into the cured salmon fillet, and wrap in plastic wrap until ready to slice.

Mussel, apple and fennel salad

1 bulb fennel, stalks removed but reserved

1 small brown onion, roughly chopped

300 ml (10 fl oz) white wine

1 kg (2 lb 3 oz) fresh mussels in the shell, rinsed well in cold water

1 tablespoon very good cider or white wine vinegar

2 tablespoons extra-virgin olive oil

1 green apple

1 shallot, very finely diced (brunoise)

salt and pepper

1 cup roughly torn fresh bread (I like to use fresh rye bread)

light olive oil

150 g (5½ oz) crème fraîche

To make the mussel, apple and fennel salad, chop the fennel stalks. Put them in a medium heavy-based saucepan with the onion over medium heat and sweat until translucent. Add the wine and bring to the boil. Add the mussels then cover the pan with a lid. Cook over high heat, shaking the pan, until the mussels start to open. As the first ones open take them out with tongs, so they don't overcook. When all the mussels in the pan are open pour the rest into a colander set over a bowl. Discard any mussels that have not opened. Mix the mussels with the cider and extra-virgin olive oil. Shave in the fennel bulb using a mandoline or a very sharp knife. Cut the apple into fine strips and add this to the salad along with the shallot. Season with salt and pepper to taste.

Toss the bread chunks with enough light olive oil to coat and sauté in a non-stick frying pan over medium heat until golden and crisp.

To serve
Cut the salmon pastrami into thin slices, about 2 mm (⅛ in) thick (enough for 3–4 slices per person). Arrange the mussel salad across each plate and scatter on the croutons. Dip a teaspoon into very hot water and scoop a small quenelle of crème fraîche onto each plate.

See photograph on page 79.

This has been on our menu at Albert St Food & Wine since day one. Grilling the haloumi gives it a delicious smoky flavour and the sharp and sweet pickles cut through the richness of the cheese. The Greek basil adds an authentic Cypriot touch.

Serves 6

GRILLED HALOUMI, ZUCCHINI PICKLES

600 g (1 lb 5 oz) haloumi

Greek basil leaves to garnish

Zucchini pickles

500 g (1 lb 2 oz) white or green zucchini (courgettes)

1 small brown onion, thinly sliced

¼ cup salt

1 teaspoon ground turmeric

145 g (5 oz/⅔ cup) caster (superfine) sugar

375 ml (12½ fl oz/1½ cups) white wine vinegar

2 teaspoons yellow mustard seeds

½ teaspoon mustard powder

To make the pickles, slice the zucchini very thinly and mix with the onion and salt. Allow to steep for an hour then rinse well in cold water three times and drain well through a colander. Transfer to a bowl.

Combine the turmeric with the sugar then combine with the rest of the ingredients in a saucepan over medium heat. Bring to the boil and pour over the zucchini and onion mixture. Cover with baking paper and allow to cool down before refrigerating.

Preheat a chargrill pan or barbecue plate to very hot.

Cut the haloumi into 1.5 cm (½ in) slices. Place the slices on the grill and cook on each side for 2-3 minutes or until distinctive lines are charred onto the cheese.

Serve the haloumi while hot, with little piles of the pickles on top and the basil leaves scattered over.

Clockwise from top right: Grilled peach, witlof, burrata, balsamic, hazelnuts (page 146); Bresaola, truffled parsnip remoulade, semolina crackers (page 88); Prawn and saffron arancini, black aïoli (page 76); Ancient grain salad, goat's curd, pomegranate, crispy fried shallots (page 140); Crudités, condiments, walnut skordalia (page 98); Fresh broad bean falafels, tahini yoghurt (page 70); Rainbow trout rillettes, rye, cucumber and watercress sandwiches (page 90); Grilled haloumi, zucchini pickles (page 82)

This dish is one of my favourites. Creamy, garlicky, salty fish with this 'divine' sauce really is a combination made in heaven. Serve it individually as pictured, or heat the baccala in a nice baking dish until golden and bubbly then serve with the bread and sauce separately and encourage your guests to dig in.

Serves 8–10 generously

BRUSCHETTA, BACCALA, GREEN GODDESS SAUCE

Baccala

500 g (1 lb 2 oz) baccala (salted cod) soaked in cold water for 2 days, water changed several times

1 large floury potato, peeled and sliced

2 sprigs of thyme

1 bay leaf

8 garlic cloves, crushed

1 litre (34 fl oz/4 cups) milk

80 g (2¾ oz) butter

75 g (2¾ oz/½ cup) plain (all-purpose) flour

2 egg yolks

60 ml (2 fl oz/¼ cup) extra-virgin olive oil

white pepper and salt

Green goddess sauce

1 small hot green chilli

2 long mild green chillies

1 x 335 g (12 oz) jar artichokes in oil, drained

2 garlic cloves, crushed

2 tablespoons salted capers, soaked in cold water for several hours then rinsed well

175 g (6 oz/1 cup) green olives, pitted

juice and zest of 1 lemon

15 g (½ oz/½ cup) roughly chopped flat-leaf (Italian) parsley

Cut the baccala into chunks. Place the fish, potato, thyme, bay leaf, garlic and milk into a large heavy-based saucepan. Poach over medium heat until the potato slices are cooked and the fish flakes easily. Strain the mixture through a colander, reserving the poaching liquid. Set aside 800 ml (27 fl oz) of the liquid and keep warm.

Remove the thyme and bay leaf and put the fish and potato mixture into a food processor. Pulse until roughly puréed.

Make a béchamel sauce (see page 46) with the butter, flour and the reserved poaching liquid. Add the warm béchamel to the food processor and pulse again to combine. Add the egg yolks and the extra-virgin olive oil and give it a few more pulses. Season with white pepper and salt if you think it needs it, remembering the fish is quite salty.

To make the green goddess sauce, split the chillies and remove the seeds. Split the drained artichoke and squeeze out any extra oil and reserve. Sear the chillies and artichoke in a chargrill pan or on a barbecue until slightly blackened.

Put all the dressing ingredients, except the parsley, into a food processor and pulse until you have a rough purée. Finally, add the parsley and enough of the reserved artichoke oil to give a nice shiny texture.

To serve

Slice a nice crusty loaf of white bread, such as ciabatta, into slices. Grill (broil) or toast the bread then spread liberally with the baccala and flash under a hot grill until golden and bubbly. Serve with the green goddess sauce on the side.

I had a starter in a bistro in London years ago that inspired this dish. A salad of finely shredded celeriac with truffled mayonnaise served with super-thin slices of 'Jambon de Paris' (a French version of prosciutto). So delicious! I've replaced the celeriac with sweeter parsnip for fun, and also because the beef bresaola has a more savoury flavour than the jambon.

Serves 6

BRESAOLA, TRUFFLED PARSNIP REMOULADE, SEMOLINA CRACKERS

about 4 very thin slices bresaola per person

Remoulade

2 large parsnips

60 g (2 oz) Mayonnaise (see page 52)

chopped black truffle (as much as you can afford, within reason!)

salt and pepper

Semolina crackers

100 g (3½ oz) semolina, plus extra for dusting

150 g (5½ oz/1 cup) self-raising flour

1 teaspoon salt

150 ml (5 fl oz) soda water (club soda) or sparkling mineral water

1 teaspoon olive oil

Preheat the oven to 180°C (350°F).

To make the semolina crackers, place the semolina, flour and salt in a bowl and make a well in the centre. Pour in the soda water and the oil and, using your fingers, mix the ingredients together to form a firm, malleable dough. Knead briefly then wrap in plastic wrap and leave to rest for about an hour.

Cut the dough into six 30 x 4 cm (12 x 1½ in) pieces and roll each piece out very thinly either using a pasta machine or a rolling pin and lots of muscle!

Put the dough onto a baking tray and bake for 5 minutes then remove from the oven and flip the crackers over. Return to the oven and bake for another 5 minutes or until golden and crisp.

For the remoulade, peel the parsnips and, using a mandoline, slice them into thin slices and then into thin strips. Toss with the mayonnaise and truffle and adjust the seasoning to taste.

To serve
Break up each cracker into two bite-sized pieces. Decoratively place the bresaola onto each cracker then top with a tangle of the remoulade. Top with extra pieces of shaved black truffle.

The combinations here are ever so posh. Cucumber and watercress sandwiches with smoked rainbow trout. Perfect after a spot of tennis, lazing on the porch with a nice G and T. Remember these little freshwater trout have delicate flesh and very fine bones. This makes them fiddly but relatively easy to fillet compared to bigger fish.

Serves 6

RAINBOW TROUT RILLETTES, RYE, CUCUMBER AND WATERCRESS SANDWICHES

For the rillettes

1. Using a razor-sharp knife, make an incision in each fresh rainbow trout from the back of the head to past the front fin. Then, first run the knife down the spine from the head going down towards the tail. Reverse the knife and zip back up towards the head.

2. Cut through the rib cage and remove the fillet.

Rillettes

2 x 300 g (10½ oz) whole rainbow trout, filleted

1 x 300 g (10½ oz) smoked rainbow trout, skinned and flaked (you can ask your fishmonger to fillet the fish for you)

salt and pepper

100 g (3½ oz) unsalted butter, at room temperature

100 g (3½ oz) plain yoghurt, at room temperature

1 egg yolk

400 ml (13½ fl oz) freshly squeezed lemon juice

500 ml (17 fl oz/2 cups) extra-virgin olive oil

1 tablespoon chopped chives

1 tablespoon grated fresh horseradish

1 loaf rye bread (the best you can find)

2 small Lebanese (short) cucumbers

100 g (3½ oz) soft butter

1 bunch of watercress, leaves picked and washed

3. Because the flesh is so soft and delicate, don't flip the fish over as you would for a more robust beast. Simply make an incision at the tail end and run your knife up the spine, keeping the blade flat and close to the bone and remove the whole skeleton, including the head. Then slide the knife under the rib bones, removing as little flesh as possible.

4. Pin-bone the fresh trout using fish tweezers, being very careful to remove all bones.

5. Preheat the oven to 160°C (320°F). Place a piece of baking paper on a baking tray. Arrange the 4 fish fillets skin side down on top. Add a few tablespoons of water and some seasoning. Cover with foil and place in the oven for 4–5 minutes. The fish should be rare at the thickest point. Allow to cool.

6. Drain off the excess juice. Turn the fillets over and peel off the skin, then remove any dark flesh.

7. Tear the fish into small pieces or flake with a fork.

5

6

7

8. Put the butter and yoghurt in a mixing bowl and hand-whisk until the mixture becomes fluffy. Alternatively, you can use an electric mixer or food processor.

9. Add the egg yolk and a little of the lemon juice. Drizzle in the extra-virgin olive oil and then add the rest of the lemon juice

8
9

10. Fold through the flaked fish, chives and horseradish. Test for seasoning and add salt and pepper to taste, then set aside.

11. Slice the rye bread thinly. Thinly slice the cucumbers and season lightly with salt so the cucumber wilts slightly. Butter the bread generously and layer on the cucumber and watercress. Cut the sandwiches into random lengths and serve alongside the rillettes.

To serve
12. Encourage your guests to thickly spread the rillettes onto the sandwiches and eat with their fingers.

I would be joyfully overwhelmed if this was put in front of me, and in my element! This is a testament to the care and love I think should go into cooking for others. It's soulful 'cooking' – even though, ironically, all the elements are raw. It's a celebration of seasonality, freshness and the primal fun of using your fingers and sharing food. Dig in with gusto knowing it's all healthy as well.

Serves 6–8

CRUDITÉS, CONDIMENTS, WALNUT SKORDALIA

Roasted garlic purée

3 garlic bulbs

olive oil

pinch of salt

Walnut skordalia

25 g (1 oz) white bread

200 ml (7 fl oz) full-cream (whole) milk

150 g (5½ oz/1½ cups) walnuts

½ garlic clove

1 teaspoon Roasted garlic purée (see method)

1¼ tablespoons freshly squeezed lemon juice

1 teaspoon extra-virgin olive oil

pinch of salt

Crudités

a combination of colourful, seasonal vegetables for your platter, such as fennel, dutch carrots, small multicoloured heirloom radishes, green beans, witlof (Belgian endive/chicory), cauliflower, celery hearts or small tomatoes – select at least 6–8 pieces per person

Condiments

black aïoli (see page 77), green goddess sauce (see page 87), tahini yoghurt (see page 72)

Preheat the oven to 160°C (320°F).

To make the roasted garlic purée, slice the tops off the garlic bulbs to expose the cloves. Drizzle with olive oil and a pinch of salt, wrap loosely in aluminium foil and seal shut.

Place the package of garlic on a bed of rock salt to insulate the heat and bake for 40 minutes or until the garlic cloves start to pop up out of their skins. Be careful not to over-roast the garlic as it will turn bitter.

Allow to cool slightly, just enough to be able to touch and squeeze out all the garlic cloves from their bulbs. Press through a fine sieve into a paste. (Store with plastic wrap in contact with the surface area of the paste in an airtight container.)

To make the walnut skordalia, remove the crusts from the bread and leave to soak in the milk.

Combine the walnuts, garlic, garlic purée and lemon juice in a food processor. Add the milk and bread mixture and process until smooth and combined. Poor in the oil, season with salt and process again.

Clean and discard all traces of dirt from the vegetables using a sharp, pointed knife and cold running water. Select the sweetest, most tender, cleanest inner parts of the produce.

If preferred, very lightly blanch some of the hardier vegetables, such as the cauliflower, green beans or fennel.

To serve

Arrange your chosen vegetables randomly and decoratively along a serving platter and serve with the dips alongside. Serve with grilled crusty bread.

SOUPS

Having a good repertoire when it comes to soups will stand you in good stead, both when entertaining and feeding the family. I often start a dinner with a little cup of something delicious to get the taste buds going. In summer a gazpacho (page 104) or a chilled pea soup (page 110), or in spring an asparagus velouté or a carrot soup with scallop and amaretti biscuit crumbs (page 112). In winter I will often serve a soup as the main meal – something hearty and filling, like my pumpkin, barley and pancetta (page 114) or steaming bowls of green vegetable soup with lots of basil pesto and crusty bread (page 116). Soups are the ultimate comfort food. Soothing or invigorating, served as an 'amuse bouche' before a meal, as a first course or a snack, they are one of my favourite things to make, eat and serve. My ideal lunch would be a fabulous soup, a simple salad, good bread and a glass of wine. What more could you want?

Although gazpacho originates from Spain, I've Frenchified this testament to the glory of ripe tomatoes to make it more my own. This very Mediterranean soup is summer in a bowl. The sweet crab, jewels of sherry jelly and avocado make this an extravagant and sophisticated starter on a warm night. Serve with a chilled Fino to take it halfway back to España.

Serves 6

HEIRLOOM TOMATO GAZPACHO, CRAB, AVOCADO, FINO SHERRY JELLY

1. Place all the vegetables, the garlic and the chilli into a blender or food processor and process until they are all well combined but not too smooth.

500 g (1 lb 2 oz) mixed ripe heirloom tomatoes

1 red capsicum (bell pepper), deseeded and chopped

1 Lebanese (short) cucumber, peeled and chopped

1 small red onion, peeled and chopped

1 small garlic clove, peeled

½ red bird's eye chilli, deseeded

80 g (2¾ oz) fresh bread, crust removed (ciabatta or good-quality white sourdough)

2 egg yolks

1 tablespoon sherry vinegar

2 tablespoons extra-virgin olive oil

salt and pepper

100 ml (3½ fl oz) fino sherry

1 leaf gold-strength gelatine, soaked in cold water

200 g (7 oz) cooked crabmeat (I use spanner crab, available raw or cooked from good fish suppliers)

2 teaspoons freshly squeezed lemon or lime juice

To serve

250 g (9 oz) mixed mini heirloom tomatoes

1 baby cucumber

1 perfect avocado

basil shoots

2. Tear the bread into small pieces. Place it in a bowl and pour over the puréed vegetable mixture. Leave to soak for 20–30 minutes or until the bread becomes mushy. Put the bread and vegetable mixture back into the blender and process again until smooth.

1	1
1	2

3. Push the mixture through a strainer into a pitcher or bowl.

4. Put the egg yolks and sherry vinegar in a bowl and whisk well. Drizzle in the extra-virgin olive oil very gradually, continuing to whisk, until you have a mayonnaise.

5. Now slowly pour in the puréed vegetable mixture, whisking continuously, until combined. Season with salt and pepper and a little more sherry vinegar if you think it needs it. Set aside and keep cool in the refrigerator until serving (remove from the refrigerator 1 hour before serving).

6. Warm the fino sherry in a small saucepan over low heat until just warm enough to dissolve the gelatine (hot to the touch, but not bubbling). Squeeze the excess water from the gelatine and add the gelatine to the sherry. Swirl to dissolve the gelatine then pour the mixture into a shallow container and refrigerate to set.

7. If you are using uncooked crabmeat, first cook it gently in a little olive oil over medium heat for about 2–3 minutes, until opaque. Season the crab with salt and pepper and some lemon or lime juice.

To serve

8. Randomly cut up the mini heirloom tomatoes and slice the baby cucumber and avocado. Divide the crabmeat into serving bowls. Arrange the tomatoes, cucumber and avocado decoratively over the top. Spoon some little bits of the fino sherry jelly around the bowl and scatter over some basil shoots. Pour the cooled gazpacho around the garnish and serve.

3
4
6

I think the title 'minted mermaid' speaks for itself. Who would have thought that a chilled, herbaceous green soup could beat a line-up of meat (predominately pork and lamb) dishes in a competition? Well this little lady romped it home with 'best in show' at Taste of Melbourne, much to the amazement of my colleagues who tried to talk me out of submitting it as a contender. Cool, clean and sexy, this soup is a true crowd pleaser.

Serves 6–8

'MINTED MERMAID'

COOL PEA SOUP, SMOKED SALMON, MINT

1 small all-purpose potato, preferably desiree, peeled and very thinly sliced

500 ml (17 fl oz/2 cups) Chicken stock (see page 34) or water

500 ml (17 fl oz/2 cups) thickened (whipping) cream

1 small leek, white part only, thinly sliced

50 g (1¾ oz) butter

500 g (1 lb 2 oz/3¼ cups) frozen peas

10 g (¼ oz/½ cup) firmly packed mint leaves

salt and white pepper

Salmon cream

120 ml (4 fl oz) thickened (whipping) cream

90 g (3 oz/⅓ cup) crème fraîche

150 g (5½ oz) smoked salmon, sliced and diced

salt and pepper

squeeze of fresh lemon juice

To serve

salmon roe

tiny peas from 200 g (7 oz) sugar snap peas

tiny mint leaves

pea tendrils (optional)

Put the potato in a saucepan with the stock and cream and bring to a simmer over medium heat.

Meanwhile, sweat the leek in the butter in a heavy-based saucepan over medium heat, until soft but not coloured. Add the peas. By this time the potato should be cooked in the cream and stock mixture. Add this to the leek and peas and add the mint. Simmer briefly then process in a blender.

Push the mixture through a sieve. Allow to cool completely then season with salt and white pepper.

For the salmon cream, whip the cream and the crème fraîche together until thick. Fold the smoked salmon through the mixture. Season with salt and pepper and a squeeze of lemon. Refrigerate until needed.

To serve
Divide the soup into 6–8 serving bowls. Using a spoon dipped in hot water, form generous quenelles of the salmon cream and add to each bowl. Spoon about a teaspoon of salmon roe around each quenelle. Sprinkle on the tiny peas and mint leaves. Garnish with the pea tendrils, if using, and serve.

This is a souped-up (so to speak) version of 'Sauce Jacqueline'. Traditionally made from carrots, sauternes and sometimes ginger, this sweet, delicate sauce usually accompanies fish and scallops. Conceptually similar, I've replaced the sauternes with Vin Santo (an Italian dessert wine) and the ginger element first made me consider gingernut biscuits (cookies) for a crunch. Then it occurred to me; Italians dip amaretti biscuits in Vin Santo …

Serves 4

CARROT AND CHERVIL SOUP, ROASTED SCALLOPS, VIN SANTO, AMARETTI

1 small all-purpose potato, preferably desiree, peeled and very thinly sliced

500 ml (17 fl oz/2 cups) Chicken stock (see page 34) or water

500 ml (17 fl oz/2 cups) thickened (whipping) cream

1 leek, white part only, thinly sliced

1 small brown onion, thinly sliced

100 g (3½ oz) butter

500 g (1 lb 2 oz) carrots, peeled and grated

2 teaspoons sugar

170 ml (5½ fl oz/⅔ cup) Vin Santo (Italian sweet dessert wine)

1 bunch of chervil stalks, washed

salt and white pepper

12 fresh scallops, no coral, dried on paper towel

12 amaretti biscuits (cookies), roughly broken

thoroughly picked sprigs of chervil for garnish

Put the potato in a saucepan with the stock and cream and bring to a simmer over medium heat.

Meanwhile, sweat the leek and onion in the butter in a heavy-based saucepan over medium heat, until soft but not coloured. Add the carrots and continue to sweat until most of the moisture has evaporated. This will take some time. Sprinkle on the sugar and 150 ml (5 fl oz) of the Vin Santo. and reduce until all the moisture has gone again. By this time the potato should be cooked in the stock and cream. Add this to the carrot mixture. Add the chervil stalks then remove the pan from the heat.

Put the soup in a blender and process very thoroughly in small batches then push through a fine sieve. Season with salt and white pepper and add the rest of the Vin Santo.

Heat a non-stick frying pan over medium heat until nearly smoking. Season the scallops with a sprinkle of salt. Sear them on their flattest side until nice and golden. Flip them onto paper towel.

To serve
Divide the soup into warm bowls. Place one whole scallop and two scallops torn in half per bowl. Sprinkle on some crushed amaretti biscuit and garnish with chervil sprigs. Serve immediately.

This recipe has multiple influences. My mum used to make a fabulous celery and potato soup that she would garnish with chopped hardboiled egg so I suppose the initial inspiration for this bowl is obvious. I remember enjoying a potato and smoked eel salad topped with an egg poached in red wine in France too. I've also made this with parsnip instead of celeriac. This soup has an amazing unctuous mouthfeel and is very rich and satisfying so design the rest of the meal keeping this in mind.

Serves 6 generously

CELERIAC SOUP, POACHED EGG, SMOKED EEL

1 smoked eel (350–400 g/12½–14 oz), filleted and skinned (reserve the bones and skin)

600 ml (20½ fl oz) milk

600 ml (20½ fl oz) Chicken stock (see page 34) or water

2 large sprigs of thyme

1 garlic clove, crushed

1 small all-purpose potato, preferably desiree, peeled and very thinly sliced

100 g (3½ oz) butter

1 small brown onion, peeled and very thinly sliced

500 g (1 lb 2 oz) celeriac, peeled, quartered and grated

3 inner stalks of celery, including leaves

120 ml (4 fl oz) white vinegar

6–8 very fresh eggs (you only need 6 but have 2 extra in case some break)

celery salt

extra-virgin olive oil

Red wine reduction

½ bottle (375 ml/12½ fl oz/1½ cups) good-quality red wine

1 tablespoon sugar

Place the eel, bones and skin in a saucepan. Add the milk, stock, thyme and garlic. Bring to the boil; reduce the heat and simmer for 10 minutes. Turn off the heat and allow to infuse for 30 minutes. Strain into another saucepan, reserving the eel. Discard the skin and bones. Add the potato and simmer until it is soft.

Meanwhile, melt the butter in a saucepan and sweat the onion until soft but not coloured. Add the celeriac and cook, stirring often, until soft enough to mash with the back of a spoon, 8–10 minutes. Add the milk and potato mixture and simmer over medium heat for 5 minutes. Transfer the mixture to a blender and process until very smooth. Push the mixture through a fine sieve.

Pick the leaves from the celery and reserve. Thinly slice the stalks and blanch in boiling salted water for 1 minute. Drain and set aside. Break the eel into small pieces (3 small nuggets for each person).

Bring a large saucepan full of water to the boil. Add the vinegar. Break the eggs into individual cups. Reduce the heat of the water to a rolling boil. Swirl the water with a slotted spoon to create a gentle whirlpool. Gently tip in 3 eggs (one at a time) and poach for about 1½ minutes. Gently remove the eggs and drain on a tray lined with paper towel. Repeat this with the remaining eggs. Keep them warm until serving.

To make the red wine reduction, stir the wine and sugar in a saucepan over medium heat until reduced to a syrupy consistency, 10–15 minutes.

To serve

Reheat the soup and check the seasoning. Put a poached egg into each warmed bowl. Scatter on some celery and the pieces of eel. Divide the hot soup into the bowls, sprinkle with celery salt, the celery leaves and drizzle in some of the red wine reduction. Serve immediately.

A meal in itself, this hearty concoction of aromatic vegetables, herbs, earthy lentils and mini pork meatballs will warm the soul on a winter's night. Make plenty as, not only will your guests want seconds, but it also freezes beautifully.

Serves 6–8

PUY LENTIL SOUP, TINY MEATBALLS, SALSA VERDE

120 ml (4 fl oz) extra-virgin olive oil

1 brown onion, peeled and finely diced

1 large carrot, peeled and finely diced

1 leek, white part only, finely diced

1 celeriac, peeled and finely diced

1 bulb fennel

1 bunch flat-leaf (Italian) parsley, stalks finely chopped and leaves chopped and reserved

3 sprigs of thyme

1 bay leaf

500 g (1 lb 2 oz) puy (tiny blue-green) or black lentils

2–3 litres (68–101 fl oz/8–12 cups) Chicken stock (see page 34)

salt and pepper

4 pork and fennel sausages or pork sausages

Salsa verde

1 bunch of curly parsley, leaves picked

6 garlic cloves

1 teaspoon salt

2 anchovy fillets

60 g (2 oz/¼ cup) capers

finely grated zest of 1 lemon,

250 ml (8½ fl oz/1 cup) extra-virgin olive oil

Heat a broad-based saucepan over medium heat, add the extra-virgin olive oil and all the vegetables, the chopped parsley stalks, thyme and the bay leaf. Sweat these off, stirring often, until fragrant and just starting to colour, 3–4 minutes. Add the lentils and the stock and bring to the boil. Reduce the heat to a simmer then cook for about an hour or until the lentils are tender. Season with salt and pepper.

To make the meatballs, squeeze dice-sized pieces of meat out of the sausage skins (you will need 3–4 meatballs per person) and then shape them to form little meatballs. Heat a frying pan (preferably non-stick) and sauté the meatballs over high heat in a little olive oil, continually shaking the pan, until golden and cooked through.

To make the salsa verde, bring a deep saucepan of salted water to the boil and have a bowl of iced water at hand. Blanch the parsley for 4–5 seconds, then refresh in the iced water. Squeeze out the excess water well, then chop roughly (this makes it easier for the processor blades to get going). Put the garlic, salt, anchovies, capers and zest in a food processor and purée to a rough paste. Add the parsley and then, with the machine running, drizzle in the oil. Check the seasoning.

To serve
Reheat the soup and check the seasoning. Add the reserved chopped parsley leaves and then divide the soup into warm bowls. Add three or four meatballs per person, drizzle on some salsa verde and serve with crusty bread.

A one-pot wonder, this is a cross between a soup and a stew. The addition of barley pays homage to the awesome lamb shank and barley that I so enjoyed in all its guises when I was a kid. I still love it. Pumpkin (winter squash), parmesan and sage all get along so well and the pancetta gives it that salty meaty kick.

Serves 6

CHUNKY PUMPKIN SOUP, BARLEY, PANCETTA, PARMESAN

180–200 ml (6–7 fl oz) extra-virgin olive oil

12 sage leaves

1 brown onion, peeled and chopped into large dice

1 leek, white part only, cut into chunky rounds

1 carrot, peeled and chopped into large dice

1½ Queensland blue or hubbard pumpkins (winter squash), peeled, deseeded and roughly chopped

220 g (8 oz/1 cup) barley, soaked for 2 hours in hot water

150 g (5½ oz) Parmigiano Reggiano or Grana Padano, grated (before grating, cut off the rind and reserve)

2 litres (68 fl oz/8 cups) Chicken stock (see page 34)

salt and pepper

6–8 thick slices pancetta (flat or rolled), cut into 1 cm (½ in) pieces

Heat the extra-virgin olive oil in a broad-based saucepan over medium heat. Add the sage leaves and gently sauté, stirring with a wooden spoon, until they colour slightly, 3–4 minutes. Add the onion, leek and carrot and sauté for a few minutes until they start to colour. Add the pumpkin. Drain the barley and rinse with cold water then add to the pan. Add the reserved rind of the parmesan.

Pour in the stock and bring up to the boil. Then reduce the heat again to a simmer until the barley is cooked and the pumpkin is tender, about 20 minutes. Season well with salt and pepper.

Heat a non-stick frying pan and fry the pancetta slices, in batches, for a few minutes until crisp. Drain on paper towel.

Divide the soup into warm bowls, sprinkle with the parmesan and top with the pancetta. Alternatively place the soup in a large tureen and serve your guests at the table.

A modern version of 'soupe au Pistou'. Pistou, also known as pesto, meaning 'pounded', originates from Provence where the influences are both French and Italian. The ingredients are all very Provençale – zucchini (courgettes), kale, beans and basil all sing in summer and, along with all the garlic and parmesan, this soup will both nourish and please the taste buds.

Serves 6–8

GREEN VEGETABLE SOUP, BASIL PESTO

125 ml (4 fl oz/½ cup) extra-virgin olive oil

4 garlic cloves, crushed

1 leek, white part only, roughly chopped

1 zucchini (courgette), sliced 5 mm (¼ in) thick

1 bunch of broccolini, roughly chopped

1 bunch of cavolo nero or kale, or ½ a bunch of each, roughly chopped

2 litres (68 fl oz/8 cups) Chicken stock (see page 34) or water

200 g (7 oz) green or flat beans, or half of each, cut into 1 cm (½ in) lengths

1 bunch of spinach, leaves picked and washed

155 g (5½ oz/1 cup) fresh or frozen peas

salt and pepper

zucchini (courgette) flowers (if in season)

Basil pesto

½ cup flat-leaf (Italian) parsley leaves

1 bunch of basil, leaves picked

3 garlic cloves

80–100 ml (2½ fl oz–3½ fl oz) extra-virgin olive oil

100 g (3½ oz/⅔ cup) pine nuts

125 g (4½ oz/1¼ cups) finely grated parmesan

salt and pepper

Put the extra-virgin olive oil and garlic in a saucepan and simply bring up from cold to medium heat to infuse the garlic nicely without frying it. Add the leek and sweat for a few minutes until tender. Add the zucchini, broccolini and cavolo nero. Add the stock and bring to a simmer. Add the beans, spinach and peas and simmer for 5–10 minutes until tender. Season with salt and pepper then turn off the heat and let the soup rest for 30 minutes to develop the flavours.

To make the pesto, bring a saucepan of salted water to the boil and have a bowl of iced water at hand. Plunge the parsley and half the basil into the water and blanch for 30 seconds. Remove the leaves with a slotted spoon and refresh in the iced water. Drain the leaves and squeeze out the extra water. Chop roughly and place in a food processor with the other half of the basil, the garlic and a splash of the extra-virgin olive oil. Purée until smooth then add the pine nuts and parmesan. Pulse briefly so the pesto stays a little chunky. Add the rest of the oil. Add more oil if you think the pesto is too thick. Season with salt and pepper.

To serve
Reheat the soup and ladle generously into deep bowls. Spoon in a dollop of pesto, top with a zucchini flower (add at the last minute, if using) and serve with crusty bread.

SALADS AND STARTERS

I have a lot of fun with my little dishes. I tend
to be playful with them and add whimsy as
I do with my desserts. I hark back to the tried
and true flavour combinations with the odd
twist. When dining out I'm more inclined
to order two or three starters instead of the
standard three courses. I'm a big fan of the
degustation menu – lots of small dishes, just
three or four mouthfuls of each so you never
lose interest. I'll usually convince whoever I'm
dining with to order the starters that I don't!
Composed salads and starters are similar
to desserts in a way – quirkier and more
interesting, reliant on freshness and careful
cooking. They are to me anyway. It may seem
obvious but try not to double up on flavours
when you are designing a menu. I'm often
surprised when guests at the restaurant
order the quail followed by the chicken, or
the gazpacho then a main course involving
tomato … as a result I'll give the waiter a hard
time, though, not the customer.

This is a new version of the classic 'salad niçoise'. I use all the usual suspects here, but tweaked and beautified into a show-stopper – if I do say so myself.

Serves 6–8

BLACK TUNA NIÇOISE, PIMENTO MOUSSE, GREEN BEANS, QUAIL EGGS

1 piece of fresh tuna, about 600 g (1 lb 5 oz)

100 ml (3½ fl oz) light olive oil

salt flakes and pepper

1 olive baguette or loaf, extremely thinly sliced

12 quail eggs

200 ml (7 fl oz) white vinegar

500 g (1 lb 2 oz) fresh green beans

a few pimento strips

2 shallots, finely diced

1 tablespoon Friendly salad dressing (see page 25)

baby basil leaves

Tapenade

155 g (5½ oz/1 cup) good-quality black olives, pitted

1 tablespoon salted capers, soaked in cold water for several hours then drained well

2 anchovy fillets

2 garlic cloves, roughly chopped

10 basil leaves

1 tablespoon olive oil

1 x 25 g (1 oz) sachet or 1 tablespoon squid ink, available from good fishmongers (optional)

Pimento mousse

3 leaves (6 g/¼ oz) gelatine, soaked in cold water

325 g (11½ oz) tinned piquillo peppers (reserve 1 pepper for the garnish)

2 teaspoons sherry vinegar

¼ teaspoon cayenne pepper

salt

250 ml (8½ fl oz/1 cup) thickened (whipping) cream, softly whipped

For the tapenade

1. Place all the tapenade ingredients into a food processor and pulse until the mixture is smooth but not too aerated.

For the tuna

2. Using a long and very sharp knife, skin the tuna
following the shape of the fish, to make a nice round piece.
Remove any excess flesh from the skin and refrigerate or
freeze for another use. Carefully remove the very dark
flesh, or blood line, which is very strong in flavour and
unpleasantly bitter. Season the tuna with salt flakes
and pepper.

3. Heat a heavy-based frying pan over high heat, add the
light olive oil and sear the tuna, rolling to colour all the
way around.

4. Spread a long sheet of plastic wrap on a work surface, then top with another sheet. Spread out the tapenade on the plastic, using a spatula to spread it out to a size that matches the circumference and the width of tuna.

5. Place the tuna at one end of the tapenade and then carefully roll up the plastic, to coat the fish with the tapenade. (You may need to do some patching here and there.) Roll the plastic wrap all the way over and around the tuna then twist the ends to secure. Refrigerate until serving.

For the pimento mousse

6. Squeeze the excess water out of the gelatine leaves and dissolve them in 1 tablespoon boiling water.

7. Drain the liquid from the peppers and purée until smooth in a blender. Add the gelatine mixture while still warm. Blend to combine. Pour the mixture into a bowl and place that bowl over another larger bowl half-filled with iced water. Season the mixture with the sherry vinegar, cayenne pepper and salt and stir over the iced water until the mixture starts to thicken. Now, using a rubber spatula, fold in a third of the cream until very well combined, then gently fold in the rest. Pour into a container and refrigerate until set, about 2 hours.

For the garnish

8. Put the olive bread in a very low (80–90°C/175–195°F) oven until dried and crispy, about 1 hour.

9. Bring two saucepans of water to the boil. Add 1 tablespoon of salt to each. Have two bowls of iced water at hand. Cook the quail eggs in one of the pans for 2 minutes and 15 seconds then, using a slotted spoon, lift them out of the water and lower into the iced water. Add the vinegar and leave for 1 hour. (This will soften the shell and make them much easier to peel.)

10. Meanwhile, plunge the green beans into the other pan of boiling water for 1 minute then drain and drop into the other bowl of iced water. Drain the beans and trim off the stalk end.

11. Carefully peel the quail eggs and rinse in cold water.

To serve

12. Cut the beans lengthways, but randomly and, in a bowl, dress with the strips of pimento, the shallots and friendly dressing. Using a very long sharp knife, slice the tuna into 6–8 rounds, about 1.5 cm (½ in) thick. Clean the knife after each slice, then remove the rings of plastic wrap. Put a spoonful of pimento mousse onto each serving plate. Put a slice of tuna on each then arrange the bean salad on the side. Cut the quail eggs in half and add to the dishes. Finish with the crispy olive bread, garnish with the baby basil leaves and serve.

Christmas in Australia on a plate! Prawn (shrimp) cocktail is a favourite in summer here, and often a mainstay in the festive season. Once again I'm using fruit in a savoury dish. The rich sweetness of the melon and the creamy avocado are perfect with the yabby. The iceberg lettuce adds freshness and crunch and, of course, authenticity.

Serves 6

YABBY COCKTAIL, ROCKMELON, AVOCADO, BASIL

12 x 100–150 g (3½–5½ oz) yabbies (freshwater crayfish)

3 very young iceberg lettuces

1 ripe rockmelon (cantaloupe/netted melon), cut into quarters (one quarter reserved for the dressing)

2 perfectly ripe avocados

small basil leaves to garnish

Dressing

¼ rockmelon (cantaloupe/netted melon)

1 small red chilli, deseeded and finely chopped

10 basil leaves

100 g (3½ oz) Mayonnaise (page 52)

30 g (1 oz) dijon mustard

30 ml (1 fl oz) sherry vinegar

60 ml (2 fl oz/¼ cup) extra-virgin olive oil

salt

Tabasco (optional)

Bring a large deep saucepan of water to the boil. Kill the yabbies by placing a sharp knife between the eyes (see page 172 for instructions). Plunge the yabbies into the rapidly boiling water and cook over high heat for 1 minute. Using a large slotted spoon, remove the yabbies and spread out on a tray to cool down.

For the dressing, remove the rind from the quarter of rockmelon and chop into chunks. Put the chunks in a blender with the chilli and basil leaves. Blend on high speed until very smooth. Strain the mixture through a sieve, pressing it through with a small ladle or the back of a spoon. Combine the rockmelon mixture with the mayonnaise, mustard and vinegar and whisk together well. Whisk in the extra-virgin olive oil then season with salt and Tabasco to taste. The dressing should be sweet, salty, spicy and tangy so be brave!

Remove the outer leaves from the lettuces and break apart the inner leaves. Peel and cut the remaining rockmelon into decorative slices

Break the heads off the yabbies and then break off the claws (see page 173 for instructions). Crack the claws with the back of a knife and gently ease out the meat. Peel the tails by gently squeezing the shell until it cracks slightly, peel off the shell then ease out the meat. Remove any intestinal tract. Cut the tails in half lengthways or diagonally or both. Halve the avocados, remove the stone and then quarter the halves. Take off the skin, trying to keep the flesh as neat as possible.

To serve
Arrange the ingredients on each serving plate and drizzle generously with the dressing. Scatter around the small basil leaves and serve.

Panzanella is a summer salad made with chunks of stale bread, usually involving ripe tomatoes, vinegar and lots of olive oil. The bread soaks up the juices and the result is delicious. I've replaced the summer with autumn ingredients with great success. Reminiscent of the forest floor, this recipe, or a version of it, is always on my menu during mushroom season.

Serves 4

GRILLED QUAIL, MUSHROOM PANZANELLA, JERUSALEM ARTICHOKE

4 x 200–250 g (7–9 oz) quails

mustard greens or chive tips to garnish

Jerusalem artichoke purée

500 g (1 lb 2 oz) Jerusalem artichokes, washed and grated

80 g (2¾ oz) butter

200 ml (7 fl oz) thickened (whipping) cream

salt and pepper

Mushroom panzanella

1 loaf ciabatta or sourdough bread

extra-virgin olive oil

a mixture of mushrooms such as pine mushrooms, slippery Jacks, king browns and oyster (about 1 cup mushrooms per person)

salt and pepper

black truffle (optional)

truffle oil

sherry or Banyuls wine vinegar

Place the quails, breast side down, on a cutting board. Using poultry shears, snip along the spine starting at the cavity end. Cut down both sides then pull to remove the backbone and neck. Using the tip of a sharp knife, carefully remove the thigh bones. Cut around the rib cage on both sides and remove the shoulder bones and wish bone. Hold the breast and gently tear out the ribs and breast plate.

For the Jerusalem artichoke purée, in a large heavy-based saucepan over medium heat, sweat the artichoke in the butter until it starts to soften. Cover with a lid and turn the heat down to low. Cook for 5 minutes or until you can easily squash the artichoke with your fingers. Add the cream and let it bubble for a few minutes. Purée well in a blender and season with salt and pepper.

For the panzanella, remove the crusts and tear the bread into chunks. Toss the bread with enough extra-virgin olive oil to coat well. Heat a non-stick frying pan over medium heat and fry the bread until golden and crunchy.

Slice the mushrooms if large or leave whole if small. (A combination of slices, wedges and whole is nice for a rustic effect.) Sauté the mushrooms in the frying pan over medium heat, seasoning separately as you go. Grate some black truffle into the mushrooms, if using, or drizzle in a few drops of truffle oil. Use both if you like, remembering that they have a very strong flavour.

Jerusalem artichoke chips

3 Jerusalem artichokes

500 ml (17 fl oz/2 cups) canola or vegetable oil

salt

Sauce

approximately 400 ml (13½ fl oz) Double chicken stock (see page 38)

1 large thyme sprig

80 g (2¾ oz) butter

salt and pepper

For the Jerusalem artichoke chips, using a mandoline or sharp knife, slice the artichoke very thinly and deep-fry at 180°C (350°F) (or until the handle of a wooden spoon bubbles vigorously when dipped in the oil) for a minute or two in the oil or until crisp. Season the chips with salt and drain on paper towel.

For the quails, season the birds on both sides and either grill or pan-fry, over medium heat skin side down, for 2 minutes then flip over and cook for a further minute.

For the sauce, put the stock and thyme in a saucepan and, over medium heat, cook until the stock is reduced by half and a syrupy consistency. While still on the heat, whisk in the butter and season with salt and pepper. Remove from the heat and set aside.

Toss the mushrooms and bread together with a little vinegar and check the seasoning.

To serve
Generously smear some Jerusalem artichoke purée on each plate then top with the mushroom panzanella. Split the quails in two and arrange over the mushrooms. Drizzle on some sauce, sprinkle over the chips and mustard greens or chive tips and serve.

See photograph on page 138.

Grilled quail, mushroom panzanella,
Jerusalem artichoke, page 136

Ancient grain salad, goat's curd, pomegranate,
crispy fried shallots, page 140

The idea here is hardly original. The combination of ingredients is age-old. Grains, pulses, pistachio nuts, pomegranate and goat's curd are all quite Middle Eastern in origin. This is a delicious and nutritious dish to serve as either a shared starter or a side dish.

Serves 6–8

ANCIENT GRAIN SALAD, GOAT'S CURD, POMEGRANATE, CRISPY FRIED SHALLOTS

100 g (3½ oz) wild rice

150 g (5½ oz) freekeh

200 g (7 oz/1 cup) red or white quinoa

100 ml (3½ fl oz) olive oil

salt and pepper

240 g (8½ oz) tinned cooked puy (tiny blue-green) lentils

400 g (14 oz) tinned chickpeas (garbanzo beans)

1 pomegranate

½ bunch dill fronds, roughly chopped

15 mint leaves, torn

60 g (2 oz) pistachio nuts, crushed

100 g (3½ oz) goat's curd

Wash the wild rice, freekeh and quinoa separately and well under cold running water. Put the wild rice in a saucepan covered with plenty of water, bring to the boil and leave to simmer for 40 minutes or until cooked but firm. Drain and spread out on a tray to cool down.

Heat some olive oil in a large heavy-based saucepan over medium heat. Add the freekeh and toast the grains, mixing to coat, for several minutes. Pour in 400 ml (13½ fl oz) boiling water, ¾ teaspoon salt and some black pepper, bring to a gentle simmer then cover and cook over a low heat for 1 hour. Make sure the freekeh is al dente then remove the lid to allow any remaining liquid to evaporate. Remove from the heat and allow to cool.

Combine the washed quinoa and 500 ml (17 fl oz/2 cups) cold water with salt and pepper in a saucepan, covered, then bring to the boil over high heat and boil for 5 minutes. Remove the lid and turn down to medium–low heat, stirring occasionally. Cook for 10 minutes or until most of the water has absorbed and the quinoa is al dente. Transfer to a tray, evenly spread the quinoa across the tray and allow to cool. When cool, mix all the grains through with your fingertips lightly, to separate them.

Rinse the lentils and chickpeas thoroughly under cold running water. Drain well, combine with the grains and mix evenly. Refrigerate.

Score through the skin of the pomegranate in half (base to head), just enough to twist the fruit apart into two chunks. Detach the seeds from the pith by holding each half, seed side down, in the palm of your hand and tapping around the skin with your knuckles or a spoon, letting the seeds fall away through your fingers into a bowl. Sift through the pomegranate and remove any white membrane.

Pomegranate dressing

60 ml (2 fl oz/¼ cup) tarragon vinegar

65 ml (2¼ fl oz) lime juice

80 ml (2½ fl oz/⅓ cup) pomegranate molasses

1 tablespoon dijon mustard

60 g (2 oz) fresh ginger, roughly chopped

salt and pepper

375 ml (12½ fl oz/1½ cups) extra-virgin olive oil

Crispy fried shallots

3 shallots, peeled

cornflour (cornstarch) to coat

500 ml (17 fl oz/2 cups) canola oil

salt

For the pomegranate dressing, combine all the ingredients in a food processor, except the extra-virgin olive oil. With the food processor running, slowly pour in the oil gradually, until smooth and emulsified. Drain through a fine sieve and set aside.

For the crispy fried shallots, very thinly slice the shallots into rounds and separate into individual rings. Coat the shallots well with cornflour, then put them into a sieve and shake off the excess cornflour. Put the oil in a suacepan and when the temperature is 150°C (300°F), or when the oil bubbles vigorously when the handle of a wooden spoon is inserted, fry the shallots until golden and crispy. Drain on paper towel and season immediately with salt.

To serve
Add the herbs, pistachio nuts and pomegranate seeds to the grains and legumes. Mix through the dressing and season. Garnish with dollops of goat's curds and some crispy fried shallots.

See photograph on page 139.

As a chef and adventurous eater I have many stories about steak tartare. I once ordered it in a brasserie in Paris to be asked by the sanctimonious waiter, 'Do you realise Mademoiselle, it is raw?'. And it has been ordered 'well-done' by customers at numerous establishments over the years. A mainstay on my menu, our customers are encouraged to smash the bread in half and use it to scoop up the yolky, meaty goodness.

Serves 6–8

STEAK TARTARE

700 g (1 lb 9 oz) beef fillet (tenderloin)

30 g (1 oz) capers, finely chopped

30 g (1 oz) cornichons, finely chopped

30 g (1 oz) shallots, finely chopped

2 tablespoons finely chopped flat-leaf (Italian) parsley

20 ml (¾ fl oz) extra-virgin olive oil

1 large thick baguette

2 tablespoons light olive oil

1 egg yolk per person

mustard cress to garnish (optional)

freshly ground black pepper

Sauce

100 g (3½ oz) dijon mustard

100 ml (3½ fl oz) tomato sauce (ketchup)

1 tablespoon Worcestershire sauce

5 drops of Tabasco

1 tablespoon cognac

salt and freshly ground black pepper

Using a very sharp knife, trim the excess fat and sinew from the meat, wiping away any excess moisture on the surface, then slice lengthways into about 5 mm (¼ in) slices. Cut the slices into strips, then cut the strips into very small dice.

For the sauce, combine all the ingredients except the salt and pepper and mix well with a whisk. Season well.

Place the meat, capers, cornichons, shallots and parsley into a bowl. Add the sauce a few tablespoons at a time until the tartare is nicely coated. Taste for seasoning and adjust if you think it needs more. Drizzle in the extra-virgin olive oil to give the mixture a lovely shine.

Cut each slice of baguette on an angle to about 2 cm (¾ in) thick. Making sure the slice of bread is also wide enough, take a small 3 cm (1¼ in) round pastry cutter and remove a circle from the centre of each piece. Heat a non-stick frying pan, add the light olive oil and toast one side over medium heat pressing the bread down slightly to make sure you have an even, flush surface of bread to pan. Flip the bread to toast the other side and season the top. Add a drop more oil, then gently place an egg yolk inside the hole, sealing it off quickly (this only takes seconds) so as not to break the yolk when you lift out the toast with a spatula. Depending on the size of your pan try not to overcrowd and stick to just toasting 2 at a time.

To serve, divide the beef fillet mix into even portions and neatly spoon a tight rectangle onto each plate. Place the yolk toast on top and decorate with mustard cress or smudged whole capers. Drizzle around a little extra-virgin olive oil and freshly ground black pepper on the yolk. Serve with a bottle of Tabasco and salt and pepper.

The choice of tomatoes available these days is amazing – black Russians, oxheart and zebra striped are just a few of the varieties you can now buy or grow. I love the juicy tomatoes and sweet watermelon juxtaposed with the salty, herby feta. The rice adds a nutty crunch and the shallots add gentle acidity and more pink!

Serves 6–8

HEIRLOOM TOMATOES, PICKLED SHALLOTS, PURSLANE, PUFFED RICE

3 shallots, thinly sliced

40 g (1½ oz) wild rice

1 litre (34 fl oz/4 cups) canola oil

½ bunch of basil, leaves picked

200 ml (7 fl oz) extra-virgin olive oil

1 kg (2 lb 3 oz) tomatoes – a nice colourful mix of heirloom and truss

¼ watermelon

salt and pepper

150 ml (5 fl oz) Pomegranate dressing (see page 141)

1 bunch of purslane

250 g (9 oz) marinated Persian feta

Pickling liquid

100 g (3½ oz) caster (superfine) sugar

100 ml (3½ fl oz) white wine vinegar

100 ml (3½ fl oz) water

1 teaspoon salt

4 allspice berries

1 teaspoon black peppercorns

Put all the pickling liquid ingredients into a small saucepan and bring to the boil over medium heat. Strain through a sieve and add the sliced shallots to the hot liquid. Steep for a minimum of 1 hour, then strain.

Deep-fry the wild rice in the oil at 200°C (400°F) until puffed. Drain on paper towel. Set aside to cool.

Have a bowl of iced water at hand and a slotted spoon. Blanch the basil leaves in salted boiling water for 30 seconds and then plunge into the iced water. Drain and squeeze out as much excess water as you can. Blend the basil well in a food processor. Add the extra-virgin olive oil and combine.

Roughly slice the tomatoes and watermelon randomly and toss in a bowl with salt and pepper and the pomegranate dressing.

To serve
Arrange the tomato and watermelon mix onto plates. Top with the purslane, crumbled feta chunks, wild rice puffs and pickled shallots. Drizzle with the basil oil.

Even though this salad doesn't involve tomatoes, it is a kind of tribute to the great Italian 'insalata caprese'. Tomatoes are, after all, a fruit, and peaches have a similar texture and tang. The burrata (a fresh cream-filled mozzarella), basil and balsamic all hark back to the classic from Capri, but the smokiness from the grill and the hazelnuts turn it into something new.

Serves 4

GRILLED PEACH, WITLOF, BURRATA, BALSAMIC, HAZELNUTS

4 perfectly ripe yellow peaches

3 witlof (Belgian endive/chicory), leaves separated

½ bunch of basil, roughly torn

4 balls of burrata

100 g (3½ oz) hazelnuts, roasted, skinned and roughly chopped

aged balsamic vinegar

black salt (optional, available from specialist food stores)

Peach dressing

2 ripe yellow peaches

1 teaspoon dijon mustard

50 ml (1¾ fl oz) sherry vinegar

5 basil leaves

salt and pepper

150 ml (5 fl oz) extra-virgin olive oil

For the dressing, peel the peaches and combine in a food processor with the dijon, vinegar, basil, salt and pepper. With the food processor running, slowly add the extra-virgin olive oil until the dressing is creamy and emulsified.

Cut the peaches in half and remove the stones. Place in a griddle or chargrill pan and grill, flesh side down, until marked with grill lines.

To serve
Dollop some dressing on each plate and stack 2 peach halves, witlof leaves and random-shaped basil leaves around and on top. Split the burrata balls in halves or thirds and arrange over the salad. Scatter over the hazelnuts and drizzle with a few drops of balsamic vinegar. Season with the black salt and serve.

From the genius of a man named Oscar Tschirky – aka 'Oscar of the Waldorf' – came the Waldorf salad. Clearly that's what I'm messing around with here. The Waldorf salad was first enjoyed in New York at the Waldorf-Astoria around 1893. Originally apple, celery, walnuts and blue cheese with a creamy dressing, I've swapped the apples for pears and celery for celeriac, but essentially the song remains the same.

Serves 6–8

WATERCRESS, PEAR AND CELERIAC SALAD, CANDIED WALNUTS, BLUE CHEESE

1 celeriac, peeled and very thinly sliced

2 perfectly ripe pears

2 witlof (Belgian endive/chicory), bases cut off and leaves separated

1 bunch watercress, leaves picked

2 inner stalks of celery, leaves removed

150–200 g (5½–7 oz) good-quality blue cheese

Candied walnuts

100 g (3½ oz) caster (superfine) sugar

100 ml (3½ fl oz) water

150 g (5½ oz/1½ cups) walnuts, roughly broken up

1 teaspoon salt flakes

Dressing

2 tablespoons dijon mustard

100 g (3½ oz) crème fraîche

juice of 1 lemon

60 ml (2 fl oz/¼ cup) walnut oil

salt and pepper

For the candied walnuts, preheat the oven to 160°C (320°F). Line a baking tray with baking paper. Put the sugar and water in a saucepan and stir with your fingers to dissolve. Brush the sugar crystals down from the side of the pan using a very clean pastry brush. Bring to the boil over medium heat and allow to bubble away, undisturbed, without stirring or shaking the pan until it reaches 118°C (244°F) on a candy thermometer.

Place the nuts in the oven to warm up. When the temperature of the sugar mixture reaches 121°C (250°F) tip in the warmed nuts and stir with a wooden spoon for several minutes until the syrup forms a candy coating around the nuts and they sound dry and crunchy. Add the salt then transfer the walnuts back onto the tray to cool.

Whisk all the dressing ingredients together well and adjust the seasoning and lemon juice to taste.

To serve
Arrange all the salad items decoratively on a serving plate and crumble on the cheese. Drizzle over the dressing and then scatter over the nuts.

PASTAS AND RISOTTOS

168
Risotto, cannellini
beans, bacon,
grilled leek, fontina

170
Marron,
chestnut and pine
mushroom risotto

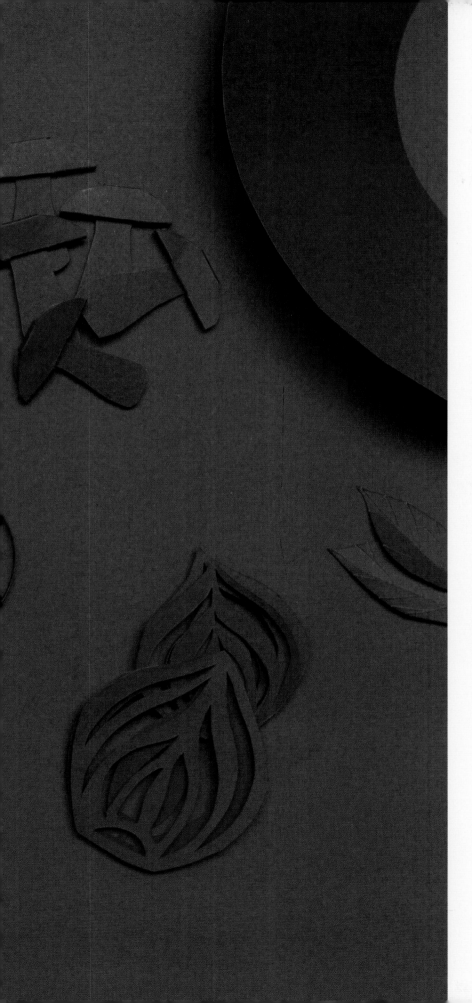

Heart-warming and filling, pastas and risottos are one-bowl wonders. I call them 'fork food' as, along with a hunk of crusty bread and a good glass of wine, a fork is all you really need to enjoy them. For impromptu gatherings, a steaming bowl of spaghetti can create a casual and fun 'help-yourself' atmosphere that I find really endearing. Once you've mastered making risotto, the combinations are endless. Try asparagus and parmesan in spring or, in summer, tomato, with lots of fresh basil and bocconcini folded through at the end. Try mushroom and taleggio in autumn and one of my favourite combinations: leek and lentil finished with crumbled blue cheese – divinely decadent! Experiment and create your own classics.

Certain combinations just make sense. Garlic, chilli, prawns (shrimp) and basil – and of course great olive oil and well-cooked pasta. My love for the Italian classic 'aglio e olio' was the initial inspiration, then I tried a quesadilla with black garlic, toasty charred corn and prawns. Sweet, spicy, herbaceous and luxurious. This is the most popular pasta dish on the menu at the restaurant.

Serves 4–6

SPAGHETTINI, PRAWNS, CHARRED CORN, GREEN CHILLI, BLACK GARLIC

salt and pepper

3 corn cobs, husks removed

6 black garlic cloves

4 garlic cloves

3 small hot green chillies, such as bird's eye or scud

300 ml (10 fl oz) extra-virgin olive oil

500 g (1 lb 2 oz) spaghettini

500 g (1 lb 2 oz) raw, peeled prawns (shrimp), deveined and chopped into small pieces

20 leaves of fresh basil

juice of 2–3 lemons

small basil leaves for garnish

Put a large saucepan of water on to boil for the pasta, and add a tablespoon of salt.

Meanwhile heat up a griddle pan or chargrill pan and grill the corn until charred on all sides, about 12 minutes. Slice the corn kernels off the cob with a very sharp knife.

Slice both garlics and the chillies very thinly and put them in another large saucepan with the extra-virgin olive oil, but don't heat it yet.

When the first pan of water is boiling, drop in the spaghettini and cook until al dente, about 4–5 minutes.

While the pasta is cooking, heat the second pan over medium heat and, when the garlic starts to bubble, add the prawn meat and stir with a wooden spoon until it is opaque.

Strain the cooked pasta and add to the other pan, along with a little of the cooking water. Add the basil and corn and toss together well. Add a little more water if the pasta is too dry. Season well with salt and pepper and plenty of lemon juice. Serve on a large platter and garnish with the small basil leaves.

Who doesn't love macaroni cheese? I've tweaked this childhood favourite by serving thick asparagus and the delightfully meaty king brown mushrooms with it. The short rigatoni, sitting upright, facilitates the addition of more cheesy sauce!

Serves 6–8

MACARONI CHEESE, KING BROWN MUSHROOMS, ASPARAGUS, TRUFFLED PECORINO

For the macaroni cheese
1. Cook the pasta at a rolling boil until al dente, about 12 minutes.
Drain and coat the pasta with the extra-virgin olive oil. Set aside to
cool a little.

Mushrooms and asparagus

3–4 king brown mushrooms

1 garlic clove, thinly sliced

1 thyme sprig

10 g (¼ oz) butter

extra-virgin olive oil

2 bunches of green asparagus
(about 400 g/14 oz)

Macaroni cheese

1 kg (2 lb 3 oz) ditalini rigati (a short rigatoni)

80 ml (2½ fl oz/⅓ cup) extra-virgin olive oil

1 quantity Béchamel sauce
(see page 46)

100 g (3½ oz/1 cup) grated parmesan

100 g (3½ oz) fontina, grated

100 g (3½ oz) cheddar, grated

salt and white pepper

10 slices truffled pecorino or thinly sliced
mozzarella (don't use normal pecorino
as it is usually aged and has a
higher fat and oil content)

15 g (½ oz) butter, plus extra for greasing

80 ml (2½ fl oz/⅓ cup) thickened
(whipping) cream

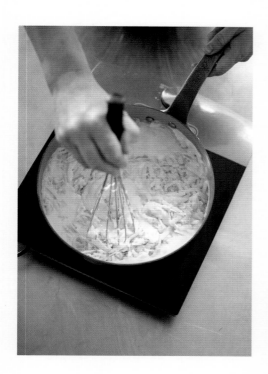

2. Prepare the béchamel sauce. Whisk the three grated cheeses into the béchamel sauce while it's still hot, until the cheese has melted through. Season with salt and white pepper.

3. Pour the béchamel sauce evenly over the macaroni and mix well until the sauce thoroughly coats the pasta.

4. Preheat the oven to 180°C (350°F). Coat a baking dish with a good smear of butter. Start placing each rigati tube, upright and randomly in the dish, until all the surface area is covered.

5. Cover the top of the rigati with the truffled pecorino slices. Dot with butter to finish and spoon over the cream randomly. Place in the oven and bake for 20 minutes, until golden brown. For the mushrooms and asparagus

6. Slice the king brown mushrooms into random shapes and cross- sections. Sauté in a shallow frying pan with the garlic, thyme, butter and a few drops of extra-virgin olive oil. over medium heat After several minutes, when the mushrooms start to colour slightly, add a splash of water, swirling the pan to create an emulsion.

7. Trim away the woody bases of the asparagus and lightly blanch in boiling water or steam for a few minutes. Add to the mushroom pan and coat with the juices.

To serve
8. Top the macaroni cheese with the asparagus and mushrooms and any remaining juices and serve with a Friendly salad (see page 25).

5
5

This is me being characteristically silly, but still keeping in mind technique and my love of the classics. When I first came across this particular pasta shape I instantly thought: 'Ha, bunny ears!'. This recipe seemed destined.

Serves 6

CAPUNTI, RABBIT BOLOGNESE, 'COTTONTAIL' SAUCE

500 g (1 lb 2 oz) capunti pasta

Bolognese

2 x 5 mm (¼ in) slices pancetta

200 ml (7 fl oz) plus 1 tablespoon light olive oil

1 brown onion, peeled and cut into very small dice or 'brunoise'

1 carrot, peeled and cut into fine dice (brunoise)

1 leek, white part only, brunoise

1 inner celery stalk, brunoise

2 king brown mushrooms, brunoise

2 garlic cloves, finely chopped

2 bay leaves

4 sprigs of thyme

½ bunch of flat-leaf (Italian) parsley, leaves picked and reserved for garnish later, half the stalks finely chopped

1 rabbit, with the liver, filleted and meat removed from bones then minced (ground) (ask your butcher to do this if you prefer)

200 g (7 oz) minced (ground) pork

375 ml (12½ fl oz/1½ cups) dry white wine

250 ml (8½ fl oz/1 cup) tomato purée or passata

Chicken stock (see page 34) to cover

salt and pepper

For the bolognese, heat a large shallow frying pan over medium heat and sweat the pancetta in the 1 tablespoon olive oil for several minutes. Add the vegetables, garlic and herbs, except for the parsley leaves. Continue to cook, without colouring, for several minutes until tender and fragrant. Tip this mixture out into a bowl and set aside.

Wipe out the pan and heat the 200 ml (7 fl oz) olive oil over high heat until hot but not smoking. Add the rabbit and pork and cook, stirring with a wooden spoon, pressing out any lumps until the meat starts to colour well all over, 6–8 minutes. (You don't want the meat to boil, you want it to colour to a nice golden brown.)

Drain the meat in a colander then return to the pan with the vegetable mixture. Return to the heat and add the wine. Cook this down until reduced by half then add the tomato purée and enough stock to cover. Reduce the heat to a simmer and let bubble, stirring often, for about 40 minutes. Season with salt and pepper. Turn off the heat and leave to rest and infuse for an hour, to develop the flavours.

'Cottontail' sauce

100 ml (3½ fl oz) thickened (whipping) cream, whipped

1 quantity freshly made Béchamel sauce (see page 46) with 80 g (2¾ oz) grated parmesan and some freshly grated nutmeg added

To serve

extra parmesan in block form

For the 'cottontail' sauce, fold the cream into the béchamel, cover with plastic wrap pressed onto the surface and set aside at room temperature.

For the pasta, bring a large deep saucepan of salted water to the boil. Boil the capunti until al dente, about 12 minutes, but test to make sure. Strain the pasta through a colander and toss with a little olive oil.

To serve
Reheat the bolognese sauce with more stock and a drizzle of olive oil if necessary, so it has a lovely, sauce-like texture. Check for seasoning. Cut the parsley leaves finely. Toss the pasta with a few hearty spoonfuls of sauce and serve onto bowl plates. Spoon on extra sauce then add a large dollop of 'cottontail' sauce to each plate. Sprinkle with parsley and shave on some parmesan. Serve.

See photograph on page 166.

Capunti, rabbit bolognese,
'cottontail' sauce, page 164

Risotto, cannellini beans, bacon,
grilled leek, fontina, page 168

I love the texture that the addition of cannellini beans gives this risotto. The smoky, charred leeks and the bacon add interest and the fontina adds rich, cheesy, melty goodness. This is an indulgent dish, not for the light-hearted or dieters!

Serves 6–8 generously (10–12 as an appetiser)

RISOTTO, CANNELLINI BEANS, BACON, GRILLED LEEK, FONTINA

1 brown onion, peeled and diced

60 ml (2 fl oz/¼ cup) extra-virgin olive oil

500 g (1 lb 2 oz/2¼ cups) arborio rice

375 ml (12½ fl oz/1½ cups) white wine

3 litres (101 fl oz/12 cups) Chicken stock (see page 34)

2 leeks, white part only

In a large heavy-based saucepan over medium heat, sauté the onion in the extra-virgin olive oil until translucent. Add the arborio rice, mix well with the onion and fry for several minutes. Deglaze the pan with the wine and reduce until the wine has evaporated. Add all the chicken stock and boil for 6 minutes.

Strain the rice through a sieve, reserving the liquid, then spread out in an even, shallow layer on a large flat tray, to cool it quickly and evenly.

Steam the leeks for 8–10 minutes until tender or until you can easily pierce them with a knife. Allow to cool and cut diagonally into 1 cm (½ in) oval discs. Heat a griddle plate or chargrill pan until very hot, and cook the leek until there are evident grill lines.

200 g (7 oz) kaiserfleisch or good-quality smoked bacon, cut into short batons (lardons)

250 g (9 oz) cooked cannellini (lima) beans (if tinned, rinse well)

200 g (7 oz) fontina, cubed with rind removed

100 g (3½ oz/1 cup) finely grated parmesan

100 ml (3½ fl oz) pouring (single/light) cream, whipped

salt and pepper

chive tips

shaved parmesan for garnish

In a heavy-based saucepan over medium heat, fry off the kaiserfleisch in a splash of olive oil for 4–5 minutes, stirring with a wooden spoon, until golden. Drain off any excess fat from the pan then add the cooked rice and enough of the reserved cooking starch to cover. Cook over medium heat, stirring all the time, for another 8 minutes or so, adding more liquid as you go until it's all absorbed – you may need to use extra chicken stock. The rice should be al dente and creamy. Add the cannellini beans and cheeses and stir well. Add half the leek discs and the whipped cream and stir vigorously to aerate the risotto. Taste for seasoning. The risotto should be quite wet but nicely emulsified. Fold through the chive tips.

To serve

Divide the risotto into warm bowls and top with the remaining leek discs tossed with a little olive oil, salt and pepper. Garnish with the shaved parmesan and serve.

See photograph on page 167.

I'm very proud when I serve this dish. There's a lot involved, but it's a labour of love so worth the effort. It's definitely for special occasions. It is a testament to beautiful, seasonal ingredients in their prime in late autumn and early winter. Serve with the best Chardonnay you can afford and a big friendly salad.

Serves 6–8

MARRON, CHESTNUT AND PINE MUSHROOM RISOTTO

1. Have a large deep saucepan of water boiling and a large bowl of iced water at hand. You will also need a big slotted spoon or long-handled tongs to remove the marrons.

2. Kill the marrons by plunging the tip of a strong knife between their eyes, through the shell.

Risotto

8 marrons or large yabbies (freshwater crayfish)	
1 onion, finely diced (brunoise)	
125 ml (4 fl oz/½ cup) extra-virgin olive oil	
600 g (1 lb 5 oz/2¾ cups) arborio rice	
2 litres (68 fl oz/8 cups) marron stock (see recipe below)	
500 g (1 lb 2 oz) chestnuts, roasted and peeled	
375 ml (12½ fl oz/1½ cups) white wine	
4–6 pine mushrooms, thinly sliced	
120 g (4½ oz) butter	
salt and pepper	
3 sprigs of tarragon	
120 g (4½ oz) mascarpone	

Marron or yabby stock

marron heads with shells on (left over from marron used for risotto above)

1 large brown onion, peeled

2 carrots, roughly chopped

1 leek, white part only, roughly chopped

4 celery stalks, roughly chopped

2 garlic cloves, roughly chopped

6 sprigs of tarragon

bouquet garni

200 ml (7 fl oz) canola or vegetable oil

2 tablespoons tomato paste (concentrated tomato purée)

60 ml (2 fl oz/¼ cup) cognac

Chicken stock (see page 34)

4 tomatoes, roughly chopped

3. Place the marrons into the rapidly boiling water for 20–30 seconds. Remove the marrons and refresh in the iced water. Holding the marrons in a cloth, as they're spiky, twist the head off each marron and set aside for later. To peel the tails, use poultry shears or very strong scissors to snip up each side of the belly shell.

4. Gently pinch near the tail end and pull to remove the shell and the intestinal tract.

5. Crack off the claws and, using the back of a knife, bash the claw to crack it slightly. Then gently pull out the bottom pincer and the main shell should slip off easily. Don't worry if you damage the flesh slightly as it's being used for risotto. (Save the shells to make the stock needed for this recipe.) Now halve the tails lengthways.

For the stock

6. Preheat the oven to 160°C (320°F). Clean out the marron heads under running water and drain. Dry out the shells and heads in the oven on a large baking tray, until all the moisture has evaporated and they start to smell nutty, 20–30 minutes. Crush the shells with a meat mallet.

7. Sauté the onion, carrot, leek, celery and garlic (the 'mirepoix') in a large heavy-based saucepan over medium heat with 3 tarragon sprigs, the bouquet garni and the oil until browned.

7

6

8. Add the marron shells to the pan and mix well. Add the tomato paste and cook out until caramelised.

9. Pour in the cognac and flambé and/or allow the alcohol to cook off before adding enough chicken stock to just cover the shells. Add the remaining 3 sprigs of tarragon and the tomatoes and simmer over low heat for 1½–2 hours.

10. Remove the pan from the heat and allow to cool naturally, so it steeps like a tea.

11. Ladle the mixture through a fine sieve and coffee filter (or a piece of muslin/cheesecloth) and let stand to settle any sediment. Gently pour out into equal portions, without disturbing the sediment. Reserve 2 litres (68 fl oz/8 cups) for this recipe and store the remainder in the freezer or refrigerator.

For the risotto

12. Have a colander or strainer at hand over a bowl or bucket to catch the liquid. Also have a large tray for cooling the rice down. In a wide, heavy-based saucepan over medium heat, sweat the onion in the extra-virgin olive oil until it just starts to turn golden. Add the rice and toast, stirring constantly, for about 3 minutes. The rice should be glossy and slightly golden. Meanwhile, have the stock on the stove warming up over medium heat.

13. Add the chestnuts (crumble them up slightly) to the rice pan then add the wine. Cook the wine out until it's all evaporated. Pour in all the stock and cook over high heat, stirring all the time, for 6 minutes. Strain and spread the rice on the tray. This will stop the rice from overcooking while you prepare the garnish. Reserve the starchy stock for later. The chestnuts should be nice and crumbly but still holding some shape.

14. Heat a frying pan over high heat and sauté the mushrooms in half of the butter and a splash of extra-virgin olive oil until lightly golden. Add a splash of water to soften and emulsify any juices then season with salt and pepper. Add the leaves from the tarragon sprigs to infuse and place into a bowl for later. Give the pan a wipe with a piece of paper towel, then return to the heat and reduce to medium.

15. Add the rest of the butter to the pan and let the butter bubble and become foamy. When the butter is nearly colouring, or 'beurre noisette', add the marron pieces and shake the pan for a few minutes to coat. Remember not to cook the marron too much as it will be incorporated into the hot rice later. Season with salt and pepper and set aside with the mushrooms and tarragon.

16. Put the rice and chestnut mixture and enough starchy stock into a large saucepan and begin cooking over medium heat, stirring all the time. Add more stock as you go and cook for about 6–8 minutes or until the rice is al dente but still quite wet in consistency (if you need additional liquid, you can use chicken stock). Fold in the other ingredients and finally the mascarpone. Check the seasoning.

To serve

17. Serve with a Friendly salad (see page 25) and crusty bread.

11

LARGE PLATES

Whether it be fish, poultry, beef, lamb or vegetarian, the main course is traditionally the focus dish of a dinner party. In restaurants the main course is generally plated individually, so when I entertain at home I like to serve the main fare on large plates or platters for my guests to share. This creates a friendly, more playful, atmosphere, very different from the formality of restaurant dining. Of course these dishes can be served individually if you prefer. Always try and source sustainable fish and happy chickens and meats; organic and free range whenever possible. We should not take the amazing produce available to us for granted, so do some research and find out where your food comes from. You'll enjoy it more if you have peace of mind.

These flavours are a little 'down Mexico way'. Mexican food is the new black here in Melbourne and everyone knows Melbournians wear a lot of black. The corn elements, along with the smoky, slippery bull horn peppers, provide an interesting textural contrast to the roasted fish and buttery sea urchin.

Serves 6

ROASTED HAPUKA, CORN PURÉE, GRILLED HORN PEPPERS, SEA URCHIN BUTTER

6 corn cobs, husks removed

150 g (5½ oz) butter

2 tablespoons crème fraîche

salt and pepper

6 green bull's horn peppers (sweet, mild green peppers)

1 bunch of spring onions (scallions) with at least 6 bulbs

1 x 720–900 g (1 lb 9 oz–2 lb) fillet hapuka or grouper, or other deep sea firm-fleshed fish, skinned and portioned into 6 x 120–150 g (4½–5½ oz) pieces

1 tablespoon light olive oil

1 portion of white polenta from Roasted rack of lamb recipe (see page 188)

chive tips to garnish

Sea urchin butter

100 g (3½ oz) fresh sea urchin meat

150 g (5½ oz) butter, softened

juice of 1 lemon

salt and pepper

To prepare the corn purée, bring a saucepan of salted water to the boil and cook 3 of the corn cobs for 2–3 minutes. Drain and allow to cool slightly. Remove the kernels with a sharp knife.

Melt half the butter in a saucepan and sweat the kernels for a few minutes over medium heat then add the crème fraîche. Season with salt and pepper then purée in a food processor. Set aside.

Heat a chargrill pan or hotplate to very hot. Slice the kernels off the other 3 corn cobs with a sharp knife, keeping them as intact as possible so you have several shards with many kernels.

Grill the peppers until charred and softened. When cool enough, peel off the skin but leave the stalks intact. Split each pepper lengthways and gently scrape out the seeds.

Trim and wash the spring onions but leave on the bulbs, making sure there is no residual dirt. Grill briefly until charred and softened.

To make the sea urchin butter, put the sea urchin in a food processor and blend until smooth. Add the butter little by little, then add the lemon juice. Season with salt and pepper. Set aside at room temperature.

Season the fish with salt and pepper. Heat a large non-stick frying pan and add the light olive oil and the remaining butter. Cook the fish over medium–high heat for 4 minutes, turning every 30 seconds until golden. Turn off the heat and allow the fish to rest while you prepare the garnish.

To serve

Warm the polenta and gently fold through the corn purée. Divide the polenta onto serving plates and garnish each with the peppers, corn kernels and spring onions. Place the fish on top then finish with a knob of sea urchin butter, garnish with chive tips and serve.

A dear friend of mine, having eaten this for the first time, said: 'This dish doesn't have a home!'. She felt it was kind of Asian but also Mediterranean and French all at the same time. A native freshwater fish, surf clams, Asian mushrooms, ginger, seaweed and locally made but Italian-style cured meat ... let's just call it an Australian dish.

Serves 6

LIGHTLY SMOKED BARRAMUNDI, CLAMS, MUSHROOMS, SEAWEED BROTH, GUANCIALE

600 g (1 lb 5 oz) fresh clams

1 tablespoon plain (all-purpose) flour

1 fillet from a 3 kg (6 lb 10 oz) fresh barramundi or a mild white-fleshed fish, such as cod or pike

10 g (¼ oz) salt

1 litre (34 fl oz/4 cups) water

2 cups hickory chips (available from barbecue supply stores)

1 bulb fennel, chopped

2 shallots, chopped

6–8 button mushrooms, sliced

1 sheet of kombu seaweed, broken into small pieces (available at Asian grocers)

40 g (1½ oz) fresh ginger, thinly sliced

50 g (1¾ oz/¼ cup) roughly crushed jasmine rice

120 ml (4 fl oz) light olive oil

3 garlic cloves, crushed

1 sprig of thyme

100 ml (3½ fl oz) dry vermouth

Purge the clams in a bucket of cold water with the flour whisked in. Agitate with your hand in the water occasionally then drain after 30 minutes.

Trim the wings and tail excess from the fish fillet and make sure there are no scales, but leave the skin on. Either portion the fillet into 6 or alternatively leave the fillet whole to serve banquet-style on a platter. Dissolve the salt in the water. Place the fish in a shallow dish and pour over the brine. Remove after 8 minutes for smaller portions or 10 minutes for the whole fillet. Drain and gently pat dry with paper towel.

Meanwhile, place the hickory chips into a heavy baking tray and place over high heat, shaking the pan, until the chips ignite, this should take about 4–5 minutes. Stir so all the chips smoulder and smoke then turn off the heat and place a wire rack over the chips. Put the fish on the rack and cover with a lid or aluminium foil. Leave to cold-smoke for 30 minutes.

In a wide-based saucepan over medium heat, sweat off the fennel, shallots, button mushrooms, seaweed, ginger and rice in the light olive oil until they start to colour slightly, about 4–5 minutes. Add the garlic and thyme then add the liquids and bring to the boil. Add the clams and cover with a lid.

Cook the clams, shaking the pan for several minutes until they start to open. As the first ones open take them out with tongs, so they don't overcook. When all the clams in the pan are open pour the rest into a colander set over a bowl. Discard any clams that have not opened. Pick the excess vegetables and ginger off the clams then set aside.

400 ml (13½ fl oz) Chicken stock (see page 34)

50 ml (1¾ fl oz) light soy sauce

salt and pepper

6-8 mushrooms per person, from a combination of Asian mushrooms, such as enoki, shimeji, shiitake and chestnut mushrooms (available from good food stores and markets), stalks trimmed

To serve

1 bunch of samphire or coriander (cilantro) sprigs

12 super-thin slices of guanciale (available from good Mediterranean food stores)

Strain the reserved broth through a very fine sieve. Check the seasoning, remembering that the clams can be quite salty.

Bring a steamer up to a simmer over low heat and put in the fish. Steam the smaller portions for 8 minutes or the larger fillet for 12 minutes.

Warm the broth in a large saucepan over low heat and add the mixed mushrooms. Bring to a simmer then add the clams to warm through.

To serve
Serve the fish in bowl plates or a deeper platter for the larger piece. Ladle over the clams and mushrooms. Garnish with the samphire or coriander and the guanciale and serve.

See photograph on page 186.

Lightly smoked barramundi, clams, mushrooms, seaweed broth, guanciale, page 184

Summer chicken cassoulet,
page 188

This is a summery, lighter version of cassoulet. Usually a very rich dish, made with confit duck or even goose, pork sausage and loads of breadcrumbs, it is a wonderful classic but this version is for the warmer months, so I use chicken, ripe tomatoes and other seasonal vegetables, along with the traditional cannellini beans.

Serves 6–8

SUMMER CHICKEN CASSOULET

Boudin blanc

2 boneless, skinless chicken breasts

salt

2 egg whites

250 ml (8½ fl oz/1 cup) thickened (whipping) cream

20 g (¾ oz) fresh tarragon, chopped

a pinch of cayenne pepper

white pepper

a few drops of truffle oil (optional)

Confit chicken

4 sprigs of thyme

1 bay leaf

6 garlic cloves

200 g (7 oz) rock salt

4 chicken leg quarters

2 kg (4 lb 6 oz) duck fat, available at good butchers and food stores

To make the boudin blanc, refrigerate the bowl of a food processor for 10 minutes. Cut the chicken fillets into about 6–8 chunks and blend in the chilled food processor with 1 teaspoon salt until smooth and shiny. Add the egg whites and continue to process until glossy.

Transfer the chicken mixture from the food processor into a large bowl and firmly stir in the cream. Add the tarragon, cayenne pepper and white pepper to taste. Add the truffle oil now, if using. Check the seasoning by wrapping a teaspoonful of the mousse in plastic wrap, like a little sausage, then tying off the ends and poaching in a saucepan of boiling water for 2–3 minutes. Unwrap and taste the boudin, and then season if necessary.

Put the chicken mixture into a piping bag with a wide nozzle. Lay four 30 cm (12 in) sheets of plastic wrap on a work surface (you can do these one at a time, if you prefer). Pipe a thick 15 cm (6 in) sausage down the centre of each piece of plastic wrap and roll up tightly. Make sure there are no air bubbles. Tie off each end.

Bring a saucepan of water to a simmer over medium heat. Poach or steam the boudin gently (simmer only, if poaching) for 5–6 minutes, then remove and allow to cool. Refrigerate until ready to serve.

To make the confit chicken, preheat the oven to 130°C (265°F). Using a mortar and pestle, pound the herbs, garlic and a little of the salt then mix with the rest of the salt. Toss the chicken leg quarters in the salt and leave to disgorge for 4 hours at room temperature. (This will draw moisture from the flesh while also imparting the flavours from the salt.) Rinse all the salt mixture off.

6 baby carrots, peeled and thickly sliced

4 banana shallots, thickly sliced

200 ml (7 fl oz) extra-virgin olive oil, or enough to cover the base of the pan well

2 sprigs of thyme

1 bay leaf

2 garlic cloves, crushed

one 3 cm (1¼ in) thick slice of kaiserfleisch or good-quality smoked bacon

300 g (10½ oz) cannellini beans, soaked overnight

2 litres (68 fl oz/8 cups) Chicken stock (see page 34)

4–6 good-quality, fragrant truss tomatoes, stalks left on

160 g (5½ oz/2 cups) fresh white breadcrumbs

leaves from 3 sprigs of tarragon, roughly chopped

100 g (3½ oz) butter, melted

salt and pepper

Melt the duck fat in a deep baking dish, add the chicken leg quarters and cover with a piece of baking paper pressed onto the surface. Cover with foil and cook for 3 hours. Allow to cool in the fat. When cool, gently remove the chicken and drain on paper towel. Cut the thighs from the legs and set aside until serving. Strain the fat into a bucket, cool to room temperature and refrigerate for next time.

Sweat the carrots and shallots in the extra-virgin olive oil until they start to colour. Add the herbs, garlic, kaiserfleisch and beans then pour over the stock. Simmer for 20–30 minutes, topping up the stock if necessary, until the beans are tender. Remove the kaiserfleisch and cut into 2 cm (¾ in) pieces.

Increase the oven temperature to 190°C (375°F). Put the chicken legs and thighs on a tray lined with baking paper and put in the oven while you prepare the rest of the ingredients.

Split the boudin diagonally and chargrill or pan-fry on the cut surface until nicely coloured. Check the seasoning of the beans remembering the confit chicken will be salty. Warm the beans with the kaiserfleisch, tomatoes and boudin pieces arranged nicely in a casserole dish or copper pan. Add the chicken legs and thighs.

Mix the breadcrumbs with the tarragon and butter and season with salt and pepper. Scatter over the cassoulet and bake for 15–20 minutes or until bubbling and the crumbs are golden.

To serve
Serve in the middle of the table with a big green salad.

See photograph on page 187.

As the name suggests, blanquette of veal is a 'white' ragout traditionally served with similarly pale sides, such as rice, noodles or potato. I'm one of those people who eats with their eyes, so I thought I would brighten up the dish with some vibrant ingredients. The musky saffron and sage butter combination, along with the broad (fava) beans, is a triumph.

Serves 6–8

BLANQUETTE OF VEAL, SAFFRON GNOCCHI, BROAD BEANS, SAGE

4 x 350–400 g (12½–14 oz) veal shanks or osso bucco

2 leeks, white part only

1 onion

4 celery stalks

4 garlic cloves, smashed

2 sprigs of sage

1 sprig of thyme

2 bay leaves

olive oil for frying

plain (all-purpose) flour for dusting

salt and white pepper

1 x 750 ml (25½ fl oz) bottle of dry white wine

2 litres (68 fl oz/8 cups) Chicken stock (see page 34)

100 g (3½ oz) unsalted butter, plus an extra knob

2 bunches of small salad or spring onions (scallions) or about 18 shallots, peeled, halved and trimmed

6–8 sage leaves

280 g (10 oz/1½ cups) peeled broad (fava) beans (blanched if fresh)

Gnocchi

1 kg (2 lb 3 oz) large floury potatoes, such as russet, desiree or sebago

1 tablespoon olive oil

a large pinch of saffron threads

100 g (3½ oz/⅔ cup) plain (all-purpose) flour

30 g (1 oz) cornflour (cornstarch)

salt and white pepper

To serve

Parmigiano Reggiano or Grana Padano

For the blanquette

1. Preheat the oven to 150°C (300°F).

2. Place the shanks in a deep saucepan and cover with cold water. Bring to the boil over high heat then pour into a colander and rinse with cold water. (This process purges any blood from the bones and means the blanquette will stay white, or 'blanc' – hence the name.)

3. Allow the shanks to dry while you prepare the 'mirepoix'. Cut the leeks, onion and celery into large thumb-sized pieces, noting that this is a braise and will be cooking for a long time so you don't want the vegetables to break down and become squishy, as this will ruin the clarity of the sauce.

4. Sweat the vegetables, garlic and herbs in olive oil over medium heat until tender, fragrant and lightly coloured.

5. Dry the shanks thoroughly on paper towel. Season some flour with salt and white pepper and roll the shanks in this, then pat off the excess.

6. Heat a heavy-based frying pan over medium heat and fry the shanks in a little oil to lightly colour them. Drain on paper towel.

7. Put the shanks and vegetables into a large flameproof casserole or baking dish over medium heat on the stovetop. Pour on the wine and let it boil down by about half. Add the chicken stock and bring back to the boil. Turn down to a simmer and lay a piece of baking paper over the surface. Either put a lid on if using a casserole or cover the baking tray with foil. Put into the oven for about 2 hours or until the meat falls easily off the bone. Let the shanks cool in the stock for at least an hour to ensure the meat stays moist and delicious.

8. Remove the shanks and take the meat off the bone. Break the meat into nice morsels, about the same size that the gnocchi will be. Reheat the braising liquid and strain it into a large saucepan. Reduce to a sauce-like consistency.

For the gnocchi

9. Put the potatoes, washed if necessary but unpeeled, into a saucepan large enough so that they aren't stacked on top of each other. Cover with cold water and bring to the boil over high heat. Reduce the heat to medium and cook until tender, until you can easily pierce the potato with a fork.

10. In a small saucepan, warm the olive oil over low heat and add the saffron. Once the saffron is warmed through add 1 tablespoon water and swirl the pan as the water evaporates. This process will leach the colour from the saffron.

11. Drain the cooked potatoes and peel them with a small knife. You will need to peel them while they're hot so use a tea towel (dish towel) to protect your hands.

12. Press the potatoes through a drum sieve directly onto a work surface, working quickly so they don't cool down.

13. Add the saffron mixture to the potato then add the flours. Season to taste.

14. Using a pastry card, chop the ingredients together until partially combined, then use your hands to bring the mixture together as a dough.

15. Knead the dough briefly. Dust your work surface with a little plain flour. Cut off portions of the dough and roll into cylinders about 3 cm (1¼ in) thick.

15 | 15
15

16. Cut and dust the gnocchi lightly with flour and put on a tray. Once all the gnocchi is made, put in the refrigerator for at least 1 hour to firm up.

16

16

17

17. In the meantime bring a deep saucepan of salted water to the boil. Have a slotted spoon and a big bowl of iced water at hand. Reduce the heat of the water to a gentle boil. Blanch the gnocchi in batches so as not to cool the water down too much.

18. When the gnocchi float to the surface, wait 30 seconds then gently remove them with the slotted spoon and drop straight into the iced water. When they are all cooked, strain into a colander and drizzle with a little olive oil. Put on a tray and set aside

19. Heat the knob of butter in a heavy-based frying pan over medium and add the onions. Sweat them off briefly then add enough water or chicken stock to cover. Put a lid on and simmer until tender.

20. Warm the sauce and meat together in a large frying pan over low heat. In another large frying pan, heat the 100 g (3½ oz) of butter over medium heat until it starts to become golden then add the sage leaves. When the sage is becoming crisp add the onions and broad beans and a splash of water or stock. Add the gnocchi and swirl to heat through. You may need to add more liquid so the gnocchi doesn't catch. Season with salt and white pepper.

To serve

21. Divide the gnocchi and vegetables onto serving plates. Spoon over the veal and sauce and scatter over the sage leaves. Using a vegetable peeler, shave some parmesan over each dish and serve.

The process of confiting duck legs in their own fat is an ancient one, used pre-refrigeration to preserve the meat. The result of this is super flavoursome and quite salty meat. I enjoy this dish when served with something leafy – cabbage, spinach or brussels sprouts are wonderful foils for the richness of the duck.

Serves 6

CONFIT DUCK LEGS, BRUSSELS SPROUTS, KAISERFLEISCH

1 garlic bulb

1 tablespoon black peppercorns

8 sprigs of thyme

1 bay leaf

1 cinnamon stick

250 g (9 oz) rock salt

6 duck legs

2.5 kg (5½ lb) duck fat, available at good butchers and food stores

1 litre (34 fl oz/4 cups) Double chicken stock (see page 38)

To prepare the duck, roughly crush the garlic, peppercorns, herbs (using only half the thyme) and cinnamon stick using a mortar and pestle then rub into the salt. Roll the duck legs in this mixture, lay flat on a tray and leave to disgorge for 4 hours. (This will draw moisture from the flesh while also imparting the flavours from the salt.) After 4 hours rinse very well in cold water. Pat dry on paper towel.

Preheat the oven to 100°C (210°F). Melt the duck fat in a deep baking dish and submerge the legs. Cover with a sheet of baking paper pressed onto the surface and then cover with aluminium foil. Cook for 4–6 hours then remove from the oven and allow to cool enough to handle. Gently remove the legs and twist out the thigh bone. Trim any unattractive bits and form into a neat shape. Refrigerate on a baking tray lined with paper until needed. (The legs will last covered like this for up to a week.) Strain the fat into a bucket and refrigerate for next time.

For the sauce, put the chicken stock, the remaining thyme and the kaiserfleisch skin in a saucepan and cook over medium heat until the liquid has reduced by about half or until a sauce-like consistency. Strain into another pan.

Trim the outer leaves from the brussels sprouts and reserve. Bring a medium saucepan of salted water to the boil and cook the whole sprouts for 6–8 minutes, depending on their size or until they are easily pierced with the tip of a knife. Drain. Cut some of the brussels sprouts in half for variation.

one 3 cm (1¼ in) thick slice of kaiserfleisch or good-quality smoked bacon, skin removed and reserved (available from continental butchers)

130 g (4½ oz) unsalted butter

200 ml (7 fl oz) canola oil

24 brussels sprouts

100 g (3½ oz) crème fraîche

1 tablespoon seeded mustard

salt and pepper

Cut the kaiserfleisch slice into 1 cm (½ in) batons or lardons. Put into a saucepan and cover with cold water. Bring up to the boil then immediately drain and spread on paper towel to dry. This removes any excess saltiness.

Increase the oven temperature to 180°C (350°F). Put the duck legs on a baking tray and brush with a little duck fat. Bake until the skin is crispy and they are heated through, about 15 minutes.

Meanwhile, melt 30 g (1 oz) of the butter in a large non-stick saucepan and add the kaiserfleisch lardons. When the lardons start to colour add the brussels sprouts and cook, shaking the pan often until the lardons are crisp and the sprouts are nicely coloured.

Heat the canola oil in a medium saucepan to 180°C (350°F) or when you dip the handle of a wooden spoon in the oil it bubbles vigorously. Fry the reserved outside leaves from the brussels sprouts for a minute or two or until the bubbling subsides. Remove with a slotted spoon and drain on paper towel. Sprinkle with salt flakes.

Bring the sauce back to the boil, allow to reduce a little and then finish by whisking in the remaining butter. Stir through the crème fraîche and seeded mustard. Check the seasoning.

To serve
Place a duck leg on each plate and spoon around the sprouts and lardons. Spoon around some sauce and top with the leaves. Serve.

See photograph on page 202.

Confit duck legs, brussels sprouts,
kaiserfleisch, page 200

Roasted rack of lamb, marjoram and parmesan crust,
melted tomato and olive sauce, white polenta, page 204

These five ingredients are the food equivalent of the answer I'd give if asked 'who would you most love to have dinner with?'. Spring lamb, olives, tomatoes, loads of garlic and the oft-neglected marjoram are a Mediterranean riot together. The white polenta soaks up the deliciousness beautifully.

Serves 6

ROASTED RACK OF LAMB, MARJORAM AND PARMESAN CRUST, MELTED TOMATO AND OLIVE SAUCE, WHITE POLENTA

3 x 6 point (600 g/1 lb 5 oz) rack of lamb, French-trimmed

salt and pepper

1 tablespoon canola or vegetable oil

Marjoram and parmesan crust

10 slices of good-quality white bread, crusts removed (about 500 g/1 lb 2 oz)

1 tablespoon fresh marjoram leaves, chopped

50 g (1¾ oz/½ cup) finely grated parmesan

1 egg yolk

200 g (7 oz) butter, softened

25 ml (1 fl oz) thickened (whipping) cream

1 teaspoon dijon mustard

salt and pepper

White polenta

1 litre (34 fl oz/4 cups) Chicken stock (see page 34)

250 g (9 oz/1⅔ cups) white polenta

100 g (3½ oz) finely grated parmesan

2 tablespoons extra-virgin olive oil

salt

To make the crust, put the bread, marjoram and parmesan in a food processor and pulse to blend. Add the egg yolk, butter, cream and mustard and blend until smooth. Season with salt and pepper.

Roll the mixture out between two sheets of baking paper to a thickness of 4 mm (¼ in). Put on a tray and refrigerate to set.

Preheat the oven to 190°C (375°F).

Season the lamb with salt and pepper. Heat a large heavy-based frying pan or a large non-stick frying pan over high heat and sear the lamb racks in the oil until lightly browned. Wrap the bones in foil so they don't burn in the oven. Set aside.

Cut the crust into slices to fit nicely on the lamb racks. Press on well and trim any overhang.

To make the polenta, bring the stock to the boil in a large saucepan and sprinkle in the polenta, whisking as you go. Cook over medium heat for 6–8 minutes until thick and creamy. Cover the surface with plastic wrap until serving.

Put the lamb racks onto a baking tray lined with foil. Put in the oven and cook for 8 minutes. Remove and allow to rest for 5 minutes before carving.

Melted tomato and olive sauce

3 garlic cloves, thinly sliced

125 ml (4 fl oz/½ cup) extra-virgin olive oil

2 sprigs of marjoram

400 g (14 oz) mixed heirloom cherry tomatoes

400 ml (13½ fl oz) Lamb stock (see page 42)

200 g (7 oz) best-quality olives, mixed colours, stored in oil not brine

40 g (1½ oz) butter

While the lamb is cooking prepare the sauce. Heat the sliced garlic in a medium saucepan in the olive oil over low heat. When it warms through, increase the heat to medium and add the marjoram and tomatoes. Swirl the pan occasionally until the tomatoes start to soften. Add the lamb stock and olives and cook until a sauce-like consistency. Add the butter and swirl to emulsify.

Return the polenta to the heat and whisk in the parmesan and the 2 tablespoons extra-virgin olive oil. Season with a little salt.

To serve
Using a very sharp knife, carve each rack into two and place on serving plates. Spoon the sauce around and serve with the polenta on the side.

See photograph on page 203.

This is a Roux brothers recipe, created when they were personal chefs to the Rothschild family in their early careers. The Rothschilds would picnic in the forest of Bois Boudran, hence the name. My version is close to the original and is very dear to me, and not just because there's lots of tarragon involved! You can substitute the chicken for quail or even fish or crayfish. I like to serve anything involving this sauce at room temperature; as it would originally have been served at a picnic.

Serves 8–10 generously

ROASTED CHICKEN, BRAISED CELERY, BOIS BOUDRAN, FINGERLING POTATOES

3 bunches of celery

250 g (9 oz) butter

4 sprigs of thyme

about 1 litre (34 fl oz/4 cups) Chicken stock (see page 34)

2 x 1.2 kg (2 lb 10 oz) chickens, trussed

salt and pepper

2 large onions, sliced into 1 cm (½ in) thick slices

1 kg (2 lb 3 oz) kipfler (fingerling) or small new potatoes

extra-virgin olive oil

chervil, chives and tarragon leaves for garnish

Bois Boudran sauce

150 ml (5 fl oz) light olive oil

50 ml (1¾ fl oz) tarragon vinegar

90 ml (3 fl oz) tomato sauce (ketchup)

1 tablespoon worcestershire sauce

5 drops of Tabasco

80 g (2¾ oz) very finely diced shallots

1 tablespoon finely chopped chives

1 tablespoon finely chopped chervil

25 g (1 oz) fresh tarragon, finely chopped

salt and pepper

To make the Bois Boudran sauce, combine all the ingredients thoroughly and adjust the seasoning. Set aside at room temperature.

Preheat the oven to 190°C (375°F). Cut the celery off about 10 cm (4 in) from the base. Remove the outer dark green stalks. Trim the base. Slice in half lengthways. Melt 100 g (3½ oz) of the butter in a flameproof baking dish and add the thyme. Place the celery, cut side down, and pour in enough stock to cover the celery. Press a piece of baking paper on the surface then cover with foil. Place in the oven while you prepare the chickens.

Rub the chicken with the remaining butter and season well with salt and pepper. Heat a large frying pan or heavy-based saucepan over medium heat. Lay in the onion slices then place the chickens on top. Add about 250 ml (8½ fl oz/1 cup) chicken stock or water and roast for 30 minutes. Check the doneness by piercing a thigh. If the juices run clear they are cooked. Invert the chickens so the cavity is upwards. Cover loosely with foil and allow to rest for 10 minutes. Remove the string from both the chickens, then carve off the legs and then the breast. Separate the legs and thighs and carve the breasts in half. Put all the pieces into a dish and spoon over the Bois Boudran sauce. Allow to marinate for at least 30 minutes at room temperature.

Remove the celery from the oven and let it cool in the stock.

Boil the potatoes in salted water until tender enough to pierce easily with the tip of a knife, about 10–15 minutes. Drain and toss with some extra-virgin olive oil.

To serve
Cut the celery again lengthways into thin slices and arrange on a platter, then add the chicken and potatoes. Spoon any excess sauce over the chicken and serve. Garnish with chervil, chives and tarragon leaves.

Clockwise from top left: Summer chicken cassoulet (page 188); Roasted chicken, braised celery, Bois Boudran, fingerling potatoes (page 206); Lightly smoked barramundi, clams, mushrooms, seaweed broth, guanciale (page 184); Roasted rib-eye, beetroot, sweet and sour onions, horseradish cream (page 210); Macaroni cheese, king brown mushrooms, asparagus, truffled pecorino (page 156)

A bit of a play with sweet and sour, this recipe is inspired by both flavour and colour; beetroot and blood, dark and light. The earthiness of the beetroot and the heat of the horseradish, offset by the sweet and sour onions, is a succulent combination with any cut of beef.

Serves 6

ROASTED RIB-EYE, BEETROOT, SWEET AND SOUR ONIONS, HORSERADISH CREAM

2 bunches (about 8–10 per bunch) of small beetroot (beets)

2 sprigs of thyme

1 bay leaf

100 ml (3½ fl oz) red wine vinegar

1 tablespoon caster (superfine) sugar

1 x 6 point rib eye steak, in one piece

salt and coarsely ground black pepper

200 ml (7 fl oz) canola oil

500 ml (17 fl oz/2 cups) Double chicken stock (see page 38)

mustard cress or watercress leaves to garnish

Sweet and sour onions

115 g (4 oz/½ cup) caster (superfine) sugar

1 x 330 g (11½ oz) jar baby pickled onions, drained and rinsed

Caramelised onions

12 baby onions

extra-virgin olive oil for brushing

145 g (5 oz/⅔ cup) caster (superfine) sugar

Trim the stalks from the beetroot and put in a saucepan with the thyme, bay leaf, vinegar and sugar. Add enough cold water to cover. Bring to the boil over medium–high heat and then turn down the heat and simmer for 15 minutes or until you can easily pierce the beetroot with the tip of a knife. Drain the liquid through a colander into another saucepan. Rub the skins off the beetroot and set aside.

For the sweet and sour onions, heat a heavy-based saucepan over medium heat and sprinkle in the sugar. Cook until golden then add the baby onions. Swirl the pan and add a splash of the beetroot cooking liquid. Remove from the heat and set aside until serving.

Preheat the oven to 200°C (400°F).

For the caramelised onions, leave the skin on and cut the onions in half, lengthways. Brush a baking tray with the extra-virgin olive oil and sprinkle with the sugar. Place the onions on the tray cut side down. Add a few tablespoons of water. Cover with foil and bake for 20 minutes or until the sugar has caramelised and the onions are tender. Allow to cool on the tray then flip over and using a small knife or scissors snip the root end and carefully remove the skin and first layer of the onions. Set aside.

Horseradish cream

1 piece of fresh horseradish, peeled and frozen (about 60 g/2 oz)

250 ml (8½ fl oz/1 cup) thickened (whipping) cream

salt and pepper

squeeze of lemon juice

For the horseradish cream, grate the frozen horseradish very finely using a microplane. Whip the cream with the horseradish until it holds stiff peaks. Season with salt and pepper and a squeeze of lemon juice. Chill until serving.

Trim the excess fat and sinew from the beef but leave some fat. Tie in between the bones with butcher's string to hold the shape while cooking. Season well with salt and black pepper.

Heat a large heavy-based frying pan over high heat and add the oil. Sear the beef all over then put into a baking tray. Roast for 20–25 minutes for medium–rare. Turn over halfway through cooking time. Remove from the oven and cover with foil. Rest the meat while you prepare the garnish.

Bring the beetroot liquid to the boil and reduce by half. Add the double chicken stock and continue to cook until it has a sauce-like consistency. Season with salt and pepper.

To serve

Add the sweet and sour onions to the sauce. Roughly separate the layers of the caramelised onions. Carve and remove the bones from the beef and reserve. Carve the fillet into six and arrange on a large, warmed serving plate. Scatter over the beetroot and onions and drizzle with the sauce. Place the bones on the platter for decoration and nibbling. Serve the horseradish cream on the side. Garnish with the mustard cress.

See photograph on page 212.

Roasted rib-eye, beetroot, sweet and sour
onions, horseradish cream, page 210

Angus beef bavette, pumpkin, caramelised witlof,
maple syrup, page 214

Once again I'm showing my love of heat with sweet. Black pepper-encrusted steak was one of my mother's signature dinner party dishes when I was growing up. I loved the way it shocked the taste buds but made your mouth water, enticing you to go back for more. The smooth sweetness of the maple-syrupy pumpkin also surprises and soothes after the peppery hit.

Serves 6

ANGUS BEEF BAVETTE, PUMPKIN, CARAMELISED WITLOF, MAPLE SYRUP

1 whole bavette (skirt/flank) steak, approximately 1.2 kg (2 lb 10 oz)

1 kensington or hubbard pumpkin (winter squash)

200 ml (7 fl oz) extra-virgin olive oil

200 ml (7 fl oz) maple syrup

1 sprig of rosemary

salt and pepper

6 witlof (Belgian endive/chicory)

black peppercorns, crushed roughly using a mortar and pestle

Clean any excess fat and sinew from the meat, then cut into 6 pieces widthways. Set aside.

Preheat the oven to 190°C (375°F).

Cut the pumpkin into quarters, scrape out the seeds and remove the skin. Reserve half for garnish. Cut the other half into chunks and toss with the extra-virgin olive oil, half the maple syrup and the rosemary. Put into a baking dish and cover with foil. Bake for 20–30 minutes until the pumpkin is very soft and slightly caramelised. Remove the sprig of rosemary. Purée the pumpkin in a blender until smooth. Season with salt and pepper. Keep warm.

Steam the rest of the pumpkin until just cooked, about 10 minutes – you should be able to pierce it easily with the tip of a knife but it should still be firm. Set aside.

Trim the outer leaves from the witlof, if damaged. Split lengthways almost all the way through and fan out. Steam, cut side down, for 10 minutes. Set aside.

Season the beef well on all sides with salt and the roughly crushed black peppercorns.

400 ml (13½ fl oz) Double chicken stock
(see page 38)

1 tablespoon thickened (whipping) cream

50 g (1¾ oz) butter, plus an extra knob

100 ml (3½ fl oz) canola oil

100 g (3½ oz/1 cup) pepitas (pumpkin seeds),
lightly roasted and salted

mustard cress for garnish

Put the stock in a saucepan and bring to the boil over medium–high heat. Reduce by half, add the cream and season well. Swirl in the butter.

Heat a large heavy-based frying pan over high to very hot. Sear the beef in half the canola oil on all sides, turning often, for 5–6 minutes for medium rare. Set aside to rest.

Meanwhile heat another heavy-based frying pan and add the remaining frying oil and the 50 g (1¾ oz) butter. Place the witlof cut-side down and cook on high heat until they start to colour. Pour the rest of the maple syrup into the pan and reduce to a glaze. Flip the witlof onto a tray and, using the same pan and the extra knob of butter, colour the pumpkin pieces and warm them through well.

To serve
Put a spoonful of pumpkin purée on each plate and arrange the witlof and pumpkin on top. Carve each steak into three and add to the plates. Drizzle the sauce around then scatter over the pepitas and mustard cress and serve.

See photograph on page 213.

The pairing of pork with apple, and apple with dates is a no-brainer, as is the addition of bread to the stuffing. Keeping the bread and other ingredients chunky is visually, as well as texturally, pleasing. The flavours mingle beautifully yet keep their integrity.

Serves 10 generously

PORCHETTA, APPLE AND DATE PANZANELLA, BUTTERED CABBAGE, DIJON MUSTARD

1 x 4 kg (8 lb 13 oz) pork loin, belly attached

salt and pepper

1 large carrot

1 garlic bulb

3 granny smith apples

1 onion

6 bay leaves

3 sprigs of thyme

olive oil

500 ml (17 fl oz/2 cups) dry apple cider

200 ml (7 fl oz) Chicken stock (see page 34)

1 small white cabbage

150 g (5½ oz) butter

1 bunch of flat-leaf (Italian) parsley,
roughly chopped

dijon mustard

Apple and date panzanella

12 small shallots, peeled

1 sprig of thyme

200–300 ml (7–10 fl oz) olive oil

Chicken stock (see page 34)

3 granny smith apples

1 loaf of ciabatta or sourdough bread,
crust removed

300 g (10½ oz) caster (superfine) sugar

50 ml (1¾ fl oz) cognac or brandy

100 ml (3½ fl oz) sherry vinegar

12 medjool dates, pitted and quartered

salt and pepper

2 pinches ground allspice

For the panzanella

1. Put the shallots in a heavy-based saucepan with the thyme and a little of the olive oil. Cook for several minutes over medium heat, until the shallots start to colour slightly. Add enough chicken stock to cover. Poach gently for about 10 minutes until you can easily pierce the shallots with the tip of a knife. Drain and set aside.

2. Peel and quarter the apples then halve the quarters.

3. Tear the bread into chunks and toss with some olive oil to coat. Toast in a non-stick frying pan over medium heat until golden and crisp.

4. Heat a heavy-based saucepan over medium heat until hot. Start to sprinkle in the sugar and, as it melts, add more, stirring with a wooden spoon constantly. When all the sugar has dissolved and has turned golden (about 3–4 minutes), add the apple pieces and toss through well. Add the cognac and the vinegar. Cook for several minutes, shaking the pan until all the sugar has dissolved.

5. Mix the bread, dates, shallots and apples together, season with salt and pepper and add the allspice.

For the meat

6. Trim the excess fat from the pork loin and season well with salt and pepper.

7. Place the panzanella close to the thick end of the pork and roll up tightly.

6
7
7

8. Using the tip of a very sharp knife, score the skin in a criss-cross fashion. Tie in 2 cm (¾ in) sections tightly with butcher's string.

7
8

9. Preheat the oven to 190°C (375°F).

10. Roughly chop the carrot, garlic, apples, onion, bay leaves and thyme and place in a heavy baking tray with the meat. Rub the meat generously with salt.

11. Add a little olive oil to the vegetables. Pour in the cider and stock and roast for 1 hour 20 minutes, then turn the oven off and open the door a fraction and allow to rest for at least 20 minutes.

12. Cut the cabbage into quarters and remove the core. Tear into bite-sized pieces.

13. Bring a saucepan of salted water to the boil. Blanch the cabbage for 5 minutes then drain into a colander. In a large frying pan melt the butter over medium heat and add the cabbage. Season well with salt and pepper and add the parsley.

To serve
14. Transfer the pork to a cutting board. Use a very sharp serated knife to cut the pork into 1.5 cm (½ in) slices. Smear a little mustard onto each plate. Divide the pork among the serving plates then garnish with the cabbage and serve. Alternatively, serve the sliced pork on a platter with the cabbage and mustard served on the side.

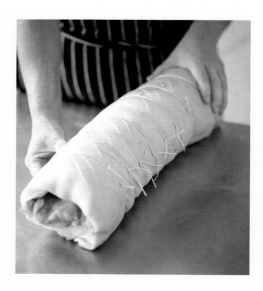

8
10

DESSERTS

It's funny that I've earned a reputation as being a pastry chef. Monikers like 'the queen of ice creams' or 'la reine des glaces', as I was known when I worked in France at La Côte Saint Jacques – a three Michelin star restaurant in Chablis. The truth is, I not only do not have a sweet tooth, but I have an obsessive aversion to sticky fingers and a topical flour allergy. However, I do love desserts – both making and watching my guests enjoy them. I have enormous fun with desserts, naming them after movie stars and pop stars – Goldie Hawn was a mango and ginger ice cream sundae with yellow rose petals and meringue 'bangs' and Iggy Popcorn a caramel, chocolate, pear and popcorn concoction that literally rocked out the door! The desserts that follow are some of my favourites and are very versatile. Don't be afraid of the technical side of things – practise, make a mess, learn from your mistakes and, most of all, have fun!

As a child, I would always request lemon delicious pudding for dessert for my birthday. I still do! This is a playful reworking of a timeless childhood favourite. As the song goes, 'You put the lime in the coconut and drink it all up'.

Serves 6

LIME AND COCONUT DELISH

120 g (4½ oz) soft butter, plus extra for greasing

250 g (9 oz) caster (superfine) sugar, plus extra for dusting

zest of 3 limes

6 eggs, separated

80 ml (2½ fl oz/⅓ cup) freshly squeezed lime juice

60 g (2 oz) self-raising flour

30 g (1 oz/½ cup) shredded coconut, plus extra for sprinkling

375 ml (12½ fl oz/1½ cups) coconut milk

Preheat the oven to 160°C (320°F). Prepare a decorative baking dish, about 600 ml (20½ fl oz) capacity, by rubbing the inside lightly with the extra butter and dusting with some of the extra sugar. Knock out the excess.

Rub the lime zest into 200 g (7 oz) of the sugar, to release the oils.

Cream the butter and zesty sugar using an electric mixer until pale and fluffy. Beat in the egg yolks gradually. Warm the lime juice slightly in a saucepan over low heat, and add bit by bit to the butter mixture until absorbed. Add the flour and shredded coconut. Mix in the coconut milk while the mixer is on low.

Whisk the egg whites until they hold soft peaks, then sprinkle on the remaining sugar and continue to whisk until the mixture is firm but not snowy. Whisk one-third of this egg white mixture into the base mixture, then fold through the rest. Pour the mixture into the baking dish. Sprinkle with extra coconut and a little sugar. Place the dish into a larger baking tray and pour in hot water to come about halfway up the side of the dish. Bake for 25–30 minutes, until golden.

To serve
Serve the delish while still hot with runny cream.

This has become my family's Christmas pudding. As we celebrate Christmas in summer in Australia, when stone fruits and berries are in all their glory and panettone graces the shelves of the Mediterranean delis, I bring these together in a festive, warm but fresh, fruity pudding more suited to our climate. Lemon verbena thrives in summer and imparts a delightful flavour that has an infinity with peaches. I suggest you get your hands on a plant.

Serves 6–8 generously

VERBENA-SCENTED BREAD AND BUTTER PUDDING, PEACHES, RASPBERRIES

250 ml (8½ fl oz/1 cup) milk

500 ml (17 fl oz/2 cups) thickened (whipping) cream, plus extra to serve

200 g (7 oz) egg yolks (about 6)

1 whole egg

150 g (5½ oz) caster (superfine) sugar, plus extra for dusting

1 cup lemon verbena leaves, plus extra for garnish

5 perfectly ripe yellow peaches

soft butter, for greasing

1 plain 750 g (1 lb 11 oz) panettone

500 g (1 lb 2 oz) fresh raspberries

Preheat the oven to 150°C (300°F).

Bring the milk and cream to the boil. Stir the egg yolks and whole egg in a heatproof bowl then add the caster sugar. Add the hot cream mixture a little at a time, whisking continuously. Scrunch the lemon verbena leaves and add to the mixture. Then remove from the heat and allow to infuse for 10–15 minutes.

Bring a saucepan of water to the boil and have a bowl of iced water at hand. Split the peaches down the middle and remove the stones. Plunge the peach halves into the boiling water briefly, then drop into the iced water. Slip off their skins and slice each half into three wedges.

Butter a 2 litre (68 fl oz/8 cup) capacity baking dish generously with soft butter, then dust with a little caster sugar. Slice the panettone and arrange in the dish. Disperse the peaches between the layers of panettone then strain over the custard mixture. Allow to soak for about 20 minutes, or until the panettone has soaked up the liquid and become quite squishy. Put the baking dish in the oven and cook for 30 minutes, or a little longer if the custard is still liquid.

To serve
Scatter the raspberries and additional lemon verbena leaves over the warm pudding and serve with some thickened cream on the side.

Everyone is familiar with crème brûlee, but for interest I like to add new elements, such as fruit and nuts. The slow-cooked, spiced quince and the honey have an ancient affinity; the cognac adds sophistication and the praline richness and texture. The pear sorbet ties it all together. Considering this is a cold dessert and the fruits are in season in the colder months, you'll find the flavours deceptively 'warm'.

Makes 6 x 140 ml (4½ fl oz) capacity moulds

HONEY AND COGNAC CASSONADE, QUINCE, CASHEW PRALINE, PEAR SORBET

Quinces

4 quinces

1 litre (34 fl oz/4 cups) water

600 g (1 lb 5 oz) caster (superfine) sugar

375 ml (12½ fl oz/1½ cups) sweet wine, such as Vin Santo, Sauternes or Muscat

1 cinnamon stick

2 strips of orange peel (peeled with a vegetable peeler, pith removed) with 1 clove stuck into each strip

Custard

50 g (1¾ oz) honey

500 ml (17 fl oz/2 cups) thickened (whipping) cream

40 g (1½ oz) caster (superfine) sugar

60 g (2 oz) egg yolks (about 3) or 1 whole egg

20 ml (¾ fl oz) cognac

Cashew praline

145 g (5 oz) salted roasted cashew nuts

1 teaspoon black sesame seeds (optional)

145 g (5 oz/⅔ cup) caster (superfine) sugar

30 ml (1 fl oz) water

Pear sorbet

6–7 large ripe pears, peeled and cored

300 g (10½ oz) caster (superfine) sugar

60 g (2 oz) powdered glucose

300 ml (10 fl oz) water

For the quinces
1. Peel, quarter and core the quinces.

2. Bring the water, sugar, wine, cinnamon stick and orange peel to the boil in a broad-based saucepan over medium heat. Add the quinces and reduce the heat to a simmer.

3. To make a cartouche, fold a sheet of baking paper large enough to fit your saucepan in half crossways, then in half again lengthways, then in half into a triangle. Trim the triangle so that it is the same length as the radius of your pan. Snip the tip off the triangle to create a hole for the steam to escape. Open out the triangle. (You can always cheat and trace around your saucepan, then cut the circle out.)

4. Cover the pan with the cartouche and place a plate on top to weight it down. Cook for 2 hours over low heat then remove the plate and continue to cook for several hours until it is a deep red colour. Turn off the heat and allow the quinces to cool in the syrup.

For the custard
5. To prepare the custard, preheat the oven to 100°C (210°F). Place the honey, cream and half the sugar into a heavy-based saucepan and bring to the boil over medium heat, stirring constantly.

6. In a mixing bowl, stir (don't whisk) the remaining sugar into the egg yolks and the whole egg. Drizzle in one-third of the hot cream mixture and stir to combine. Add the cognac and pour into a pitcher.

4

7. Prepare a baking dish or tray lined with paper towel or a tea towel (dish towel) to prevent the moulds from slipping around during cooking.

8. Slice each quince piece into quarters and arrange on the base of each mould. Place six 140 ml (4½ fl oz) capacity moulds into the baking dish and divide the mixture between the moulds to cover the fruit. Pour very hot water into the baking dish to come three-quarters of the way up the sides of the moulds. Cover the entire dish with foil and carefully place into the oven. Take care not to slosh the water into the custard. Cook for 45 minutes or until the custards wobble but look cooked. (They should not have 'souffléd' or risen at all.) Remove the custards from the water bath, then refrigerate until chilled.

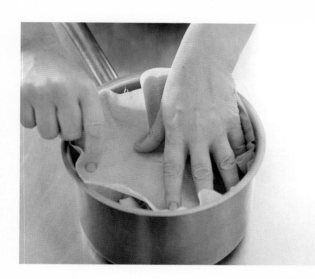

For the praline

9. Preheat the oven to 160°C (320°F) and line a baking tray with baking paper.

10. Roughly chop the nuts and put on the tray with the sesame seeds, if using, to heat briefly later.

11. Put the sugar and water in a medium-sized saucepan. Stir with your fingertips to dissolve the sugar slightly. Cook over medium heat, without stirring, until it starts to colour.

12. Place the nuts and sesame seeds in the oven to warm up. This ensures the nuts won't cool the caramel down and cause it to 'seize'.

13. Swirl the caramel in the saucepan with a spoon until golden, then tip in the nuts and sesame seeds and stir with a wooden spoon to coat completely. Tip the caramel back onto the tray now lined with baking paper, spreading the mixture out evenly, and allow to cool until hard. Crush roughly using a mortar and pestle or pulse in a food processor until crumbly.

For the sorbet

14. Roughly slice the pears. Put in a heavy-based saucepan with the other ingredients. Bring up to a simmer over medium heat and cook for 10–15 minutes with a lid on, or until the pears are tender. Allow to cool slightly. Purée the mixture in a blender then strain the mixture through a sieve using a ladle or the back of a spoon to push the mixture through. Refrigerate to chill then churn in an ice cream maker according to the manufacturer's instructions. (Churn the sorbet as close to serving as possible – no more than several hours before. This way it stays soft and spoonable.)

To serve

15. Sprinkle the praline generously over half the surface of each cassonade then, using a spoon dipped in hot water, place a quenelle of pear sorbet on the other side. Serve immediately.

Traditionally this dessert is made with cherries baked in a buttered dish covered with a thick pancake-like batter. I've lightened it up with the addition of ground nuts. This version is made with tangy blackberries, which happened to be in season at the time of photographing the book, but the variations are many. Substitute blackberries with apricots and use hazelnuts instead of pistachio nuts and serve with cream instead of ice cream. Use the poached quince from page 234 and serve with vanilla ice cream ... be creative!

Serves 6

BLACKBERRY AND PISTACHIO CLAFOUTIS, PISTACHIO ICE CREAM

Ice cream

300 ml (10 fl oz) milk

250 ml (8½ fl oz/1 cup) thickened (whipping) cream

40 g (1½ oz) pistachio nut paste (coloured and flavoured)

100 g (3½ oz) egg yolks (about 5)

55 g (2 oz/¼ cup) caster (superfine) sugar

To make the ice cream, combine the milk, cream and pistachio nut paste in a saucepan and bring to a simmer over low heat.

In a bowl, whisk the egg yolks then add the caster sugar. Continue whisking until pale and thick. Pour in one-third of the hot liquid, whisking constantly. (This tempers, or stabilises, the egg yolks. If you add all the mixture at once the yolks may curdle.) Pour the yolk mixture back into the pan and cook over medium heat, stirring constantly and slowly with a wooden spoon, using a figure-eight movement, until the mixture begins to thicken. To test whether the custard, or crème anglaise, is ready, draw a line across the back of the spoon; if a line remains visible for several seconds it is ready. If you are unsure use a candy thermometer. When the anglaise reaches 80°C (176°F) it is ready.

Pour the custard into a bowl and place over another larger bowl filled with iced water to arrest the cooking. Allow to cool completely, stirring occasionally, then strain through a fine sieve.

Churn in an ice-cream maker, according to the manufacturer's instructions. Churn the ice cream no more than several hours before serving, so it stays soft and spoonable.

Clafoutis

115 g (4 oz/½ cup) caster (superfine) sugar, plus extra for sprinkling

80 g (2¾ oz) pistachio nuts, finely ground, plus extra coarsely chopped pistachio nuts for garnish

10 g (¼ oz) plain (all-purpose) flour

2 whole eggs

60 g (2 oz) egg yolks (about 3)

250 ml (8½ fl oz/1 cup) thickened (whipping) cream

500 g (1 lb 2 oz) fresh or frozen blackberries

To make the clafoutis, mix together the dry ingredients. Whisk the whole eggs, egg yolks and cream together in a bowl then add the combined dry ingredients and mix well. Allow to rest at room temperature for several hours.

Preheat the oven to 180°C (350°F). Butter 6 individual 250–300 ml (8½–10 fl oz) baking dishes and sprinkle with caster sugar. Knock out the excess sugar. Divide the blackberries among the dishes and pour over the batter. Sprinkle with the coarsely chopped pistachio nuts and bake for about 15 minutes or until puffed up and set. Allow to cool for a couple of minutes.

To serve
Top each individual baking dish with a generous scoop of the pistachio ice cream and serve immediately.

See photograph on page 242.

Blackberry and pistachio clafoutis,
pistachio ice cream, page 240

'Hazy fantazy': Caramel parfait glacé, gianduja mousse, salted hazelnut caramel, page 244

Inspired by some of my favourite chocolate bars from when I was little, this 'kill me now' dessert never fails to induce swoons. However, to ensure none of your guests keel over, don't serve a heavy meal before it. This recipe may seem complicated but all the elements can be prepared well in advance and assembled at the last minute. Don't forget the salt!

Serves 8–10 generously

'HAZY FANTAZY'

CARAMEL PARFAIT GLACÉ, GIANDUJA MOUSSE, SALTED HAZELNUT CARAMEL

Caramel base

300 ml (10 fl oz) thickened (whipping) cream

115 g (4 oz) liquid glucose

1 vanilla bean, split and seeds scraped out

145 g (5 oz/⅔ cup) caster (superfine) sugar

50 g (1¾ oz) butter, cubed

3 x 6 g/¼ oz gold-strength gelatine leaves, soaked in iced water to soften, then squeezed to remove excess water

Bombe

50 g (1¾ oz) caster (superfine) sugar

20 g (¾ oz) liquid glucose

60 ml (2 fl oz/¼ cup) water

160 g (5½ oz) egg yolks (about 8)

200 ml (7 fl oz) thickened (whipping) cream, whipped to soft peak stage

To make the caramel base, put the cream, liquid glucose and vanilla bean and seeds in a saucepan and bring to the boil over medium heat.

Meanwhile, heat another heavy-based saucepan over medium heat until 1 teaspoon of the sugar melts when sprinkled in. Gradually add the remaining sugar and stir constantly until all the sugar has melted and is light golden brown. Be careful not to let the caramel become too dark or it will taste bitter. Slowly pour the hot cream mixture onto the caramel, whisking until combined. Whisk in the butter, then the gelatine. Strain into a stainless steel bowl and set aside to cool, whisking occasionally.

To make the bombe, put the sugar, glucose and water into a small saucepan, stirring with your fingers to dissolve the sugar slightly, then brush any crystals from the side of the pan with a pastry brush dipped in water. Bring to the boil. Continue to bubble, without stirring, until the syrup reaches 118°C (244°F) on a candy thermometer.

Meanwhile, place the egg yolks in the bowl of an electric mixer fitted with a whisk attachment and beat on medium speed to lightly break up.

Once the sugar has reached 118°C (245°F), remove from the heat and let the bubbles die down slightly. Reduce the speed of the electric mixer to medium and pour the sugar syrup down the side of the bowl into the egg yolk. Increase the speed and whisk until the mixture has cooled. Remove the bowl from the mixer and gently fold the bombe and the cooled caramel base together, then fold in the whipped cream. Pour the parfait into serving glasses and refrigerate overnight.

Milk chocolate mousse

100 g (3½ oz) best-quality couverture milk chocolate

150 g (5½ oz) gianduja (hazelnut-flavoured chocolate)

150 ml (5 fl oz) Crème anglaise (see page 62)

225 ml (7½ fl oz) thickened (whipping) cream, very softly whipped

Salted hazelnut caramel

200 ml (7 fl oz) thickened (whipping) cream

80 g (2¾ oz) liquid glucose

115 g (4 oz/½ cup) caster (superfine) sugar

50 g (1¾ oz) butter, cubed

100 g (3½ oz) roasted and peeled hazelnuts, roughly chopped

1 teaspoon salt flakes

To serve

dark chocolate plaques (8 x 4 cm/3¼ x 1½ in), broken into shards (have some spares just in case)

gold leaf (optional)

For the mousse, melt the chocolates in a large heatproof bowl placed over a saucepan of barely simmering water. Let more than half the chocolate melt before you give it a stir with a wooden spoon or rubber spatula. You want the temperature of the chocolate to be about 45°C (113°F).

Carefully warm the crème anglaise to about the same temperature as the chocolate, so when they are mixed the chocolate doesn't seize up. This is important as the chocolate will set and become unworkable if the anglaise is too cold. Add one-third of the warm anglaise to the melted chocolate. Using a rubber spatula, begin stirring the two together just in one section of the bowl to form a core of mixture (as if you were making a mayonnaise) – you are not mixing everything together. This will ensure that the chocolate doesn't split. Add half the remaining anglaise, gradually working in more of the chocolate. Now add the remaining anglaise and mix thoroughly until the mixture is smooth and shiny and looks almost elastic.

While the chocolate is still very slightly warm, add one-third of the whipped cream and quickly fold through with the spatula. Allow to cool for several minutes, then fold through the remaining whipped cream. Make sure the cream is completely incorporated. Refrigerate until needed.

To make the salted hazelnut caramel, follow the method for making the caramel parfait opposite, until the stage where the butter is whisked in. Then fold through the hazelnuts and salt and keep at room temperature.

To serve

Using a spoon dipped in very hot water, form a ball of the mousse and place carefully on top of each parfait in the serving glasses. Spoon on some hazelnut caramel and some shards of chocolate plaque. If you are feeling decadent, use some gold leaf to finish.

See photograph on page 243.

Clockwise from top left: Lime and coconut delish (page 228); Verbena-scented bread and butter pudding, peaches, raspberries (page 230); Blackberry and pistachio clafoutis, pistachio ice cream (page 240); Mango, mandarin, passionfruit; fromage frais sorbet, lemongrass syrup (page 260)

This is my version of Escoffier's Poire Belle Hélène – poached pear with vanilla ice cream and chocolate sauce. My version has all the elements of the great chef's classic – dark chocolate, poached pear and rich vanilla ice cream – but made into a tart. The light but decadent chocolate filling in the buttery pastry adds texture and crunch.

Serves 12

NEW CLASSIC 'BELLE HÉLÈNE'

For the ice cream

1. Combine the milk, cream and vanilla bean and seeds in a saucepan over medium heat and bring to a simmer.

2. In a large bowl whisk the egg yolks with the sugar until pale and thick. Pour in one-third of the hot milk and cream mixture, whisking constantly. Whisk in the rest

Ice cream

250 ml (8½ fl oz/1 cup) milk

250 ml (8½ fl oz/1 cup) thickened (whipping) cream

1 vanilla bean, split and seeds scraped out

100 g (3½ oz) egg yolks (about 5)

100 g (3½ oz) caster (superfine) sugar

Pears

750 g (1 lb 11 oz) caster (superfine) sugar

1.5 litres (51 fl oz/6 cups) water

6 william, bartlett or packham pears, in between hard and ripe (very ripe fruit will become soft and squishy when poached and rock hard fruit will stay too firm and discolour)

Pastry

half a quantity of the Pâte sucrée recipe (see page 56)

Filling

420 g (15 oz) dark couverture chocolate, as féves (buttons) or finely grated

300 g (10½ oz) butter, at room temperature

3 whole eggs

4 egg yolks

55 g (2 oz/¼ cup) caster (superfine) sugar

then return the mixture to the saucepan. Over medium heat, stir constantly with a wooden spoon using a figure-eight movement until the mixture starts to thicken. To test whether the custard is ready, lift the spoon from the pan and run your finger across the back of it; if the line remains distinct for several seconds it's ready. If you're unsure, use a candy thermometer and when the temperature reaches 80°C (176°F), it's ready.

3. Pour the custard into a bowl and place it over a larger bowl half-filled with iced water to arrest the cooking. Once it has cooled, strain through a fine sieve. No more than several hours before serving the dessert (so the ice cream is still soft and spoonable), churn in an ice cream maker according to the manufacturer's instructions.

For the pears
4. Choose a wide-based saucepan that will not crowd the fruit. Ideally the fruit should be well spaced, cut side up, while cooking. Combine the sugar and water in the saucepan over medium heat and stir to dissolve the sugar. Bring to the boil then reduce to a simmer.

5. Meanwhile, carefully peel the pears, starting at the stalk. Halve the fruit, keeping the stalks intact, and remove the core using a melon baller. Add the fruit, cut side up, to the simmering liquid and cover with a piece of baking paper cut to fit the pan. Simmer over low heat for about 15 minutes or until you can easily pierce the fruit with the tip of a knife. Using a slotted spoon, remove the pears and place on a plate or tray, cut side down, and refrigerate until serving. Reduce some of the poaching liquid down by half or until syrupy and set aside.

For the pastry
6. Preheat the oven to 180°C (350°F). Remove your pastry from the refrigerator and cut it into manageable pieces. Place the pastry on a work surface. Soften the pieces of dough by smearing each bit away from you, so they all become the same texture and more workable.

7. Bring the dough together again and shape it into a ball.

6
6 | 7

8. Gently but firmly tap out the pastry with a rolling pin.

9. Roll the dough out quickly, making one-quarter turns every couple of rolls to keep the thickness and the round shape even. Roll the pastry around the rolling pin until it is 32 cm (12¾ in) – 2 cm (¾ in) larger than the 30 cm (12 in) loose-based tart tin that it will go into.

10. Lay the pastry over the tart tin. Carefully press the pastry into the tin, taking care not to warm it up too much.

11. Roll the rolling pin over the top of the pastry in the tin, to trim off the excess.

12. Pinch up the sides of the pastry, using your left index finger and right thumb and index finger, to form a decorative rim. (This step is optional but it gives a lovely effect.) Put the tart in the freezer for 10 minutes at least to firm up.

10 | 11
| 12

13. Once the pastry is quite hard, carefully line it with foil, pressing it well into the corners and smoothing out any wrinkles.

14. Fill the tart with uncooked rice all the way up to the top. (I use rice, as opposed to beans or baking weights, as it forms more of a uniform mass that doesn't have any gaps, therefore the baked pastry will have fewer imperfections.) Slide the tart onto a baking tray and bake for about 15 minutes or until the edges are golden.

14

14

13

15. Carefully remove the foil and rice and return the tart to the oven for another 5 minutes to dry out and to even up the colour. Remove the tart shell and turn the oven down to 150°C (300°F).

30 g (1 oz) caster (superfine) sugar

60 g (2 oz) plain (all-purpose) flour, sifted

40 g (1½ oz) butter, melted and cooled

250 g (9 oz) jar raspberry, blackberry or blueberry jam (or a combination)

Poached blood plums

6 perfectly ripe blood plums

145 g (5 oz/⅔ cup) caster (superfine) sugar

500 ml (17 fl oz/2 cups) water

100 ml (3½ fl oz) raspberry juice (you should have juice left from the jelly)

zest of 1 orange, removed with a vegetable peeler, white pith removed

1 star anise

1 vanilla bean, split and seeds scraped out

To serve

250 g (9 oz) raspberries

250 g (9 oz) blackberries

250 g (9 oz) blueberries

silver leaf (optional)

the egg white mixture to the TPT mixture, along with the sifted flour and cooled melted butter. Fold the ingredients together using a spatula then fold in the rest of the egg white mixture. Spread onto the prepared baking tray and bake for 5 minutes. The cake should be light golden brown and puffed up. Remove the tray from the oven, invert the joconde and peel off the baking paper. Allow to cool.

Warm up the jam in a small saucepan over low heat with a splash of water and push through a sieve to remove the seeds. Using a pastry brush or palette knife, spread a generous layer of jam over the joconde, leaving one-quarter uncovered. Cut the joconde into 4 strips widthways, then stack on top of each other leaving the un-jammed one until last. Trim the edges. Wrap in plastic wrap and set aside until serving.

For the poached blood plums, cut the plums in half and remove the stones. Combine the other ingredients in a saucepan and bring the syrup to a simmer over medium heat and then reduce the heat to low. Add the fruit, cut side up, and cover with a cartouche (see page 236). Poach over low heat until the plums are just hot through and tender. (Take care that the syrup doesn't boil or the fruit will become too soft and fall apart.) Remove the pan from the heat and allow to cool in the syrup then remove the plums gently with a slotted spoon. Place on a plate or tray and refrigerate. Return the syrup to the heat and reduce by half. Strain and refrigerate.

To serve
Dip each dariole mould into very hot water and invert onto serving plates. Shake to dislodge. Place a slice of the joconde on each plate. Add two halves of plum each and scatter on the berries. Drizzle with a little plum syrup. Add tiny wisps of silver leaf using tweezers or the tip of a small knife.

See photograph on page 265.

INDEX

Page numbers in *italics* indicate photographs.